The God Who Answers By Fire

A Jewish Saga

BY JUNE VOLK

The God Who Answers by Fire
by June Volk

Copyright © June Volk, 2008
All Rights Reserved

Printed in Canada.

Library of Congress Catalog Card Number: 2008938780
International Standard Book Number 978-0-9794514-2-3

Cover photo by Jonathan Volk.

Cover design: Ambassador Productions, Gainesville, FL

DEDICATION

This book is dedicated with love to the
God Who answers by fire,
to my beloved husband, Shelly,
to my children: Scott, Beth, Dean, Trudy, Bill and Suzi,
to my grandchildren: Alysa, Billy, Jonathan, Benjamin, Timothy,
Joseph, Jesse, Sarah, Emily and Rachel.

ACKNOWLEDGMENTS

There are so many people I desire to thank for the days, weeks, months and years of work that went into this manuscript. First, I want to thank the Lord for allowing me to write this book of remembrance to Him and for being with me, always enlightening my mind to remember the details of the testimony written within these pages.

To my husband, Shelly, who has been my greatest encourager to complete this work and get it published. Thank you for the hours spent with me editing and proofreading this manuscript. Thank you so much for your love and dedication to me and to this book.

To my daughter-in-law, Beth, thank you for the many hours of labor you put in editing the first rough draft of this book. My use of commas and run-on sentences was unique.

Thank you to Arthur Katz, who read the rough draft and said, "I cried as I read your manuscript. It's a Jewish Saga!" Thank you, Arthur, for taking the time to read my manuscript and for your encouragement to have it published.

To my faithful brother and dear friend, David Ravenhill, for reading the rough draft and encouraging me to complete the book and to have it published, thank you.

To my Arab brother, Dr. Anis Shorrosh, who came into my office one day about nine years ago and said, "Jubilant Junie, I heard that you are writing a book! Read me your table of contents, please! Jubilant Junie, it is anointed! Get it published!" Thank you, Anis, for your encouragement.

To my dear sister and friend in Israel, Carrie, thank you for taking the time to read my first rough draft and giving me your wise guidelines for consistency. You are a wonderful journalist and adviser. Thank you for your encouragement to press on to complete this work.

Thank you to Sue Schaefer, Ginny Hanna, Peter and Joanne Brock and Vera Brennan for helping me in the final editing process.

Thank you to Chad Bergstrom for your wise advice in the final editing process.

Thank you to the Evangelical Sisters of Mary, particularly to Sister Rebecca and Sister Deborah, for allowing the name of the Sisterhood to be used.

And thank you to the Evangelical Sisters of Mary branch in Phoenix for allowing me to stay in your guest house while I worked to finalize this manuscript for the publisher.

Thank you to all my children and grandchildren who read much of this manuscript and encouraged me to complete it. Being known as Nana has been one of the greatest blessings in my life.

Thank you to each one who reads this book and takes to heart the words written within these pages.

CONTENTS

CONCLUSION

FOREWORD

According to *Webster's New World Dictionary*, one of the definitions of *blind* is, hidden from sight. I went on only one *blind* date in my life and that date turned out to be my wife, June. After just a few minutes of being with her, there was no longer any blindness; she was in perfect view, all 4'11"of her. She was beautiful and very transparent and there was something about her that touched my heart. Not being a believer at the time, I could not understand the hand of God in the relationship, but I certainly understand now the Lord's grace and love for me, bringing June into my life.

When you read this book, you will sense her love, compassion, and sensitivity to our Messiah as well as to all people. When she first accepted Jesus as her Lord, I was very jealous that there was another man in her life who was hidden from my sight, so I was unable to communicate with Him. However, after forty-four years of marriage, I am so glad for this *other* Man who has made our relationship like a three-fold cord.

This book, a compilation of life experiences with Biblical instruction, is a faith builder not just for women but for men as well. For women, it will encourage you to love and trust the Lord with all your heart. For men, I hope you will, after reading this book, appreciate your wives even more and acknowledge that you and your wife are one.

Perhaps as you read through the following pages, you might feel to scratch your head thinking that some of these vignettes are exaggerations or not even real. I testify that each and every one occurred as described as I witnessed or lived through each event.

So, if there are any *blind* spots in your life, I pray that they will become visible and that this book will create an even greater desire and passion for you to live a life of faith that will bring glory to the Name of the Lord.

Shelly Volk

INTRODUCTION

This book is divided into three parts:

PART I speaks of my affluent, independent life experiences living in New York and Connecticut before finding the God of Israel, as well as some events that followed afterward. My new faith brought about an awareness of the God Who answers by fire. This section reveals some of the changes that took place in my life as a result of that awareness. These pages are filled with experiences of God's faithfulness which is seen in how He intervened in everyday life, and met me in my personal struggles.

PART II is about God changing my heart and lifestyle. The Lord's calling my husband, Shelly, brought us to northern Minnesota. We left our beautiful home, sold or gave away most of what we owned and moved into a twelve-foot-wide trailer on a farm, to be part of a community of believers. The farm was located on an Indian reservation. The trials connected with such a dramatically different way of living are found in this section. This section also reveals the faithfulness of the Lord in everyday life. As I sought the Lord, He taught me more of His ways. Miracles, healings and victories in prayer are revealed in these pages. These eight-and-a-half years were learning years. Jesus became my Lord, and I learned to love Him more because of His love.

PART III brings us to Phoenix where life in the desert presented its own unique problems. But again, the faithfulness of the Lord brought us through them all, and I saw His hand on our lives. The congregation that Shelly pastored grew, Shelly and I were on radio and television, young people returned to the Lord, barren women conceived and broken marriages were healed. We saw the power of God through deliverance, breaking down strongholds in many lives, and we also witnessed many of our Jewish kinsmen coming to the saving knowledge of their Messiah.

This section also tells of our call to Calvary, literally and spiritually. After Shelly served at Calvary Church of The Valley for almost ten years as the Senior Pastor, we experienced betrayal and rejection from his leaders. Yet, the Lord sustained us and deepened our love for Him even more. Many poems were written during the heartbreaking events in the years that followed which are also included in this section. God was with us and He revealed Himself faithful to us through it all.

The CONCLUSION completes *The God Who Answers By Fire* with a vignette, "Where Do We Go From Here?" This describes where I find myself at this time in my life and there is also a challenge for you, the reader. "Truth Revealed" is a poem I wrote that is thought worthy. And, "To My Kinsmen With Love" is an expression of my heart, and I believe the Lord's heart as well, for my Jewish people.

Because I felt commissioned by the Lord to write this book, I wrote as I remembered His intervention. Each vignette holds its own teaching experience. I trust that you will be encouraged to know that the Lord desires to intervene in your life, as He did in mine. He desires to meet you in good times and bad times, as He met me. His life will enable you to overcome all destructive experiences as He brings healing to your heart. *He restores my soul,* from Psalm 23, has become a reality to me. He desires to restore your soul and to revive your spirit. May you be blessed as you read.

Psalm 81

SING FOR joy to God our strength;
Shout joyfully to the God of Jacob.
Raise a song, strike the timbrel,
The sweet sounding lyre with the harp.
Blow the trumpet at the new moon,
At the full moon, on our feast day.
For it is a statute for Israel,
An ordinance of the God of Jacob.
He established it for a testimony in Joseph,
When he went throughout the land of Egypt.
I heard a language that I did not know:

I relieved his shoulder of the burden,
His hands were freed from the basket.
You called in trouble, and I rescued you;
I answered you in the hiding place of thunder;
I proved you at the waters of Meribah. Selah.
Hear, O My people, and I will admonish you;
O Israel, if you would listen to Me!
Let there be no strange god among you;
Nor shall you worship any foreign god.
I, the LORD, am your God,
Who brought you up from the land of Egypt;
Open your mouth wide and I will fill it.

But My people did not listen to My voice;
And Israel did not obey Me.
So I gave them over to the stubbornness of their heart,
To walk in their own devices.
Oh that My people would listen to Me,
That Israel would walk in My ways!
I would quickly subdue their enemies,
And turn My hand against their adversaries.
Those who hate the LORD would pretend obedience to Him;
And their time of punishment would be forever.
But I would feed you with the finest of the wheat;
And with honey from the rock I would satisfy you.

Part 1

UNTIL I SAW HIS FACE

My heart says of you, "Seek his face!"
Your face, LORD, I will seek.
Psalm 27:8

It was September of 1962 when Shelly and I first met. My great Aunt Flora was married to Shelly's Uncle Nat. Aunt Flora wanted me to meet Shelly's older brother, Norman, because she thought we would make a wonderful couple. Norman was twenty-seven, I was nineteen and very excited with the possibility of dating someone so much older. Aunt Flora was visiting us from Michigan when Norman came to our home. I must confess, I thought he was very handsome and charming. However, he had a girlfriend at the time, so he told Shelly about me. Shelly called about three days later and asked me for a date. Since Norman was so handsome and charming, I thought, "Why not? His brother is a little younger, closer to my age. I'll accept!"

Shelly was to meet me in front of 1400 Broadway, the building where I worked in New York City. He knew I would be wearing a white coat. As I waited, a beautiful black car pulled up to the curb and the warm smiling face of a young man greeted me. Shelly motioned for me to come into the car and as he opened my door from the driver's seat, he looked up and said, "You're pretty. You're really pretty." In that moment I felt as if I had known him all my life. I had never experienced feeling as comfortable with anyone. We went to a beautiful restaurant for dinner.

I opened my heart and life to Shelly that evening. I remember sharing all of my thoughts, my heart's desires, as well as my struggles. He seemed to care about everything I was saying and listened intently to every word. After dinner, we went to The Winter Garden Theater where Eddie Fisher was performing. Following the concert, we drove back to Brooklyn, talking non-stop all the way home. I did not experience a moment of awkwardness that entire evening.

Although I thought Shelly was the nicest person I had ever met, I felt he was not my type. I had my idea of what my husband would be like and he was not the one for me. So I thought! He seemed too quiet. I had a picture in my mind of how my husband would look and he did not fit the picture. The next evening after work, Shelly phoned and asked me out for Saturday night to go bowling with his neighbors. I thought, "He spent so much money on me, I should at least go out with him one more time to show my appreciation." So, I accepted the date.

When Shelly arrived Saturday evening, he had his neighbor's children with him. I could not believe it! Never did anyone make a date seem so relaxed, so natural. It was as though we were old friends, family—not a date. Before we went bowling, he took me to his parents' home to meet them. Can you imagine meeting your date's parents the second time you go out with him? This was getting a little too close for comfort because in my mind this was our last date. So I thought!

On the way home, Shelly informed me that Aunt Flora and Uncle Nat were coming for a visit in December. They wanted to take us out with Norman and his girlfriend, Linda. "Oh no," I thought, "December—that's three months away! How can I go out with him for three more months? But what will Aunt Flora think? I do not want to hurt her." I was concerned that she would be disappointed if I did not care for her nephew. I felt trapped.

We went out every weekend for the next three months. It was odd because I really liked Shelly. We always laughed together, and I told all my friends about him. I would say, "He is the nicest guy I have ever met in my life. He is just not my type."

However, the morning after each date, I would see my friend Claire and she would comment, "June, you are glowing. Are you sure you are not in love with Shelly?" I would always reply nervously, "In love with him? Are you kidding? He is not my type!" I would get extremely anxious every time I found myself thinking about how I could end our relationship. I also felt terribly guilty about going out with Shelly feeling the way I did.

December came quickly. Aunt Flora and Uncle Nat arrived from Michigan. We were together at Shelly's parents' home on Friday evening for their *Shabbat* (Sabbath) meal with our entire family. On Saturday evening, Aunt Flora and Uncle Nat took us to an exclusive restaurant and nightclub. Sunday night, our families went out for dinner. We most certainly appeared to be one big happy family! I was a nervous wreck thinking that it was almost time to end our relationship. Monday morning, Aunt Flora and Uncle Nat flew home to Michigan. Shelly and I had a date that evening to see the Broadway play, "Milk And Honey." This was going to be *the* night. My mother was very concerned about how Shelly would take the break up. She asked me to please be sensitive when I communicated my feelings.

Shelly picked me up after work, and we went for dinner and then to the play. We were not enjoying the play, so we left before it ended and went to Madison Square Garden to find Norman and Linda, who were at a basketball game. I wondered how we might find them in a crowd of thousands when suddenly, there they were walking toward us. We went to a restaurant where Linda and I excused ourselves to go to the ladies room to freshen up. Linda asked if I was planning on going out with Shelly New Year's Eve, so I informed her of my intention to end the relationship that evening.

During the drive home, I began a conversation with Shelly which lasted until four in the morning and concluded in my den. When he closed the door behind him, my mother came out of her bedroom with a cold compress on her head. She had thrown up all evening and now had a headache from imagining how Shelly would take the news of our break up. My mother asked how Shelly was and I answered, "Mom, I am going to marry him!" She was so upset with me; she turned to go back into her bedroom, mumbling under her breath, "I cannot believe this. How can you marry him with the way you feel? Are you crazy?"

As I walked slowly down the hall to my bedroom early that Tuesday morning, I realized that my heart had been changed. I could not understand how it had happened myself, yet I knew that Shelly Volk was going to ask me to marry him and I was going to say yes.

He phoned the following evening and asked if I would like to meet his cousin. I told him I would love to and he said he would pick me up in an hour. I remember staying home from work that day in celebration of my anticipated marriage-to-be. When Shelly arrived, we drove to his cousin's home and parked across the street. He began a conversation that ended with the question, "Will you marry me?" I never did get to meet his cousin that night.

We drove to his parents' home to let them know we were going to be married. His mother and father were delighted because they really loved me. I will never forget the look on Norman's face when he got home that evening. As he entered the house, his mother beamed, "Give June a big hug. She and Shelly are getting married!" I am sure Linda had told him what I had said to her the night before. Norman looked at me as if to say, "Who are you kidding?"

A few weeks later at a *Shabbat* meal, Shelly put a beautiful diamond ring in my water goblet. Everyone in the family was waiting to see how long it would take for me to find it. His mother gasped as I picked up the goblet to take a drink. My face was aglow; my heart was filled with joy, as Shelly placed the diamond engagement ring on my finger.

We decided to marry the following September and began making arrangements for the wedding. Those months before we married were wonderful, because I experienced being cherished and deeply loved by Shelly. The excitement of preparing to be a bride was one of the greatest experiences in all my life. The ceremony and reception were to be celebrated in the main ballroom of Menorah Temple, and over three-hundred invitations were in the mail.

On September 14, 1963, Shelly and I were married. That evening was the most memorable in my life other than the night that I met Jesus. I remember pacing the hall before the ceremony thinking that this was for the rest of my life. How did I know that Shelly was the right one for me? There were so many men in the world, how could I be sure? What was I doing? Once I said, "I do," that vow was made that would last for all the days of my life. "June, are you sure you know what you are doing?"

Then I heard the voice of the director of Menorah Temple calling me to take my place on the platform, behind the curtain, in the rear of the sanctuary. As I stood with my bouquet, my hands shook. My knees grew weak. The groomsmen, bridesmaids and the maid of honor were all down the aisle. The song, "This Is My Beloved," was being sung as the curtain was lifting. It was time for me to step down, but I stood there frozen. The director was behind a curtain, which was behind me and he said, "Step down." I did not move. He said again, "Step down!" I stood there frozen. Finally, he ordered in a loud firm voice, "Get out of here!" He pushed me and my foot slipped from under me. My parents grabbed my arms, and we began to walk slowly down the aisle.

I smiled, but my insides were shaking. Every eye was on me. I could hardly breathe. Fear gripped me—Until I Saw His Face. Shelly was looking at me with his strong smile of assurance. I was cherished and loved by him. All my fears disappeared. He would be my husband and take care of me all the days of my life.

❧❦

There is a song with these words: *O Lord, You're Beautiful. Your face is all I see.* Just as fear gripped my heart before I made my vow to Shelly, so in life there are many fears that we face from within and without. We experience doubts and unrest. It is not until we see His face that fear, doubt and unrest leave us. Marriage is a picture of the love God has for His people:

For thy Maker is thine husband; the LORD of hosts is his name;
and thy Redeemer the Holy One of Israel;
The God of the whole earth shall he be called.
Isaiah 54:5

If Shelly caused my doubts, fears and unrest to be settled when I saw the warm smile on his face, how much more will the Lord bring you peace within, when you see His face?

Seek His Face

And ye shall seek me, and find me,
when ye shall search for me with all your heart.
Jeremiah 29:13

FATHER, PLEASE
I REALLY WANT TO KNOW

Then you call on the name of your god,
and I will call on the name of the LORD.
The god who answers by fire—he is God.
I Kings 18:24

Ten years had passed since we were married. Our children, Scott, Dean and Suzi were born within six years of each other. Shelly had been a wonderful husband and together we treasured our children, who were truly the joy of our lives. Sharing these years together had caused my love for Shelly to grow deeper and richer.

Shelly's upbringing was filled with the richness of Jewish tradition. His mother revered the God of Israel and taught her sons to honor the Sabbath. We had a respect for God, even though He seemed to be impersonal and distant. All the holy days were observed with Shelly's parents. We joined their synagogue and attended services with Shelly's parents, his brother Norman and his wife Rita, along with Shelly's younger brother, Paul. Since my early childhood, Rita and I had been best friends and she was my maid of honor at our wedding. I had introduced her to Norman and was delighted when they fell in love and married.

The *shul* (synagogue) we attended was orthodox. Although we were not orthodox in our life style, we felt we should honor Shelly's parents by joining with them. The rabbi was a learned student of the Scriptures and also an attorney. Rabbi Rabinowitz was very close with our family and cared personally for everyone in his congregation. The services lasted longer than those of the other

7

synagogues in the neighborhood; consequently, on *Yom Kippur*, we were the last to break our fast. My parents and my brother, Robert, would join us for the meal.

During the day, before sundown of *Yom Kippur*, we prepared platters with assortments of fish, cheeses, fruits and vegetables. We made tuna fish and egg salad and garnished the bowls that held them with fancy greens and radishes. We had baskets filled with various kinds of sweet breads, *bialy* rolls (a soft roll similar to a bagel) and bagels. We also had platters with assorted cakes and Jewish pastries. Uncle Phil and Aunt Lillie would walk over to the house with their children and join us for dessert. Shelly's mother practiced her European ways and I had a deep admiration for her. Family gatherings in remembrance of the Lord were significant, so the *Yom Kippurs* we celebrated together are memories to be treasured.

Every Friday evening, our family celebrated the Sabbath at the home of Shelly's parents. There was a deep sense of reverence for the Lord present at the dinner table. Mom welcomed in the Sabbath by lighting the *Shabbat* candles and saying the blessing over them. Dad raised the *challah* (Jewish egg bread) toward heaven and said the blessing over it. After he broke the *challah* in half and took a small piece to eat, Mom would say, "*Good Shabbas*," and serve the meal. Our times together were precious and meaningful, storing up memories that are forever sealed in my heart. Scott and Dean were old enough to remember the *Shabbat* dinners at their Grandma Lily and Grandpa Sol's home.

After Shelly had graduated from college and received his degree in Economics, he began his career with a major stock brokerage firm. He became successful in his profession and was a good provider for our family. He first worked in the research department, transferring into sales after Scott was born. Within one year, Shelly was one of the leading producers in his local office. After he had been in sales for eight years, his firm promoted him to vice-president and offered him a position in management. He accepted and was given the branch office in New Haven, Connecticut, where the challenges of his new position inspired him.

We purchased a beautiful home in Orange, a suburb of New Haven. The children quickly made friends and adjusted well in school. Shelly was fulfilled in his new position and he took pleasure in our affluent lifestyle. As for me, I was experiencing a tremendous void in my life, which I could not understand. Why was I not content?

One afternoon, during a Mah Jongg game (a Chinese board game) at the country club, I looked at my friends sitting around the table and said, "Look at us, grown women playing games. What are we doing? There has to be something more meaningful to life than this." Everyone stared at me as if I was crazy and asked, "Like what?" I remember answering, "I don't know. But there has to be something more to life than this." My heart was searching for something deeper, but I had no understanding of what that *something* deeper could be.

About that time, Shelly's younger brother, Paul, moved to Berkeley, California, with three of his Jewish friends. Before relocating, he had been an instructor of philosophy at Rutgers University. Paul and his friends were intellectuals living in the fast lane. They, too, were searching for a deeper meaning to life. Despite resistance to their conventional upbringing, within two years of their quest, Paul and each of his friends came to the saving knowledge of Jesus as Messiah and the Son of God. Paul returned for a visit to New York City, so that he could tell his family of his new found faith.

We were at Shelly's parents' home when Paul attempted to share his belief in Jesus. Mom and Dad were so disturbed that they left the house. Shelly stood up, spat on the floor, picked Suzi up from her high-chair, took Scott and Dean by their hands and followed his parents out the front door. I remained in the house with Paul, who appeared to be deeply troubled over his family's reaction.

"Poor Pauly boy, he is so confused," I reasoned. Last year he told me about some guru. Two years ago he encouraged me to try drugs to spice up my life. This year, it was Jesus. I really loved Paul, so I decided to listen to what he had to say in hope that it might help him to feel better. As I sat with Paul, he read many Scriptures to me from his Bible.

I honestly cannot recall what he read, although I do remember one question he asked because Scott had asked me that very question some weeks before. He had returned home from his Hebrew School class, and I was washing dishes when he asked, "Mom, does God exist?" I remember staring into the dishwater for awhile, not knowing how to respond. I tried to answer Scott as honestly as I could at the time, "I don't know, Scott. I am not sure if anyone really does know if God exists. However, I would hope that He does."

My response to Paul was the same as it had been to Scott and he continued to question me. Taking the concept that God did exist, he asked how I envisioned Him. I pondered his question for awhile and compared God to the sun and the rays of the sun to people. "We originate with God, come down to earth, and then go back to God," I responded.

"If we take that concept as being the truth," he asked me, "do you believe that every man, woman and child that ever walked the face of the earth should believe that way?" I responded resolutely, "Of course not, Paul. Everyone has his own religion, his own belief or idea that he considers to be true. We cannot tell people that what we believe is right for them." Paul pointed his finger toward me and, with all authority, declared that he knew what he believed was right not only for him but for every man, woman and child that ever walked the face of the earth. He told me that I did not have to believe him; if I really wanted to know the truth, I could ask God. For so it is written, For whosoever shall call upon the name of the Lord shall be saved …

Just consider, if God existed and I called out to Him, He would answer me? The possibility impressed me and I determined in my heart, that one day, I would call out to the God of Israel and ask Him if Jesus was His Son. What I did not realize was that I would call out to God that very night.

While driving home from Shelly's parents, I questioned Scott and Dean about God. Shelly got upset and asked me to please end the conversation. The children fell asleep and we did not communicate much more that evening because when we arrived home, we were both exhausted and went to bed.

In the middle of the night, I was awakened by a bad dream. I sat up startled. Shelly took my hand and asked if I was alright and I told him that I was, yet I could not go back to sleep. After lying awake for a long while, I thought that this would be as good a time as any to ask God if Jesus was His Son. I somehow knew, deep within my heart, that if God did exist, the only true God was the God of Israel—the God of Abraham, Isaac and Jacob. That was the God my heart longed to know.

With that thought in mind, I cried out, "Father, if You can hear me, please answer me, was Jesus Your Son? Father, please I really want to know, was Jesus Your Son?" I looked over at my window shade and fire surrounded it. I thought, "What is happening? The shade is on fire, but it is not being consumed." I felt an extreme pressure on top of my head as the fire moved up to the border of the ceiling and encircled our entire bedroom.

In my mind, I was thinking, "This is just your imagination, June." I felt chills going up and down my legs as I was still thinking, "This is just your imagination." I then felt something enter within that cleaned up everything inside of me. I was still thinking, "This is just your imagination." My tongue started to gyrate up and down uncontrollably and out of my mouth were coming words that I was not speaking. I did not know them. I had never heard them. Those words were:

> *... Our Father which art in heaven,*
> *Hallowed be thy name.*
> *Thy kingdom come.*
> *Thy will be done in earth,*
> *as it is in heaven.*
> *Give us this day our daily bread.*
> *And forgive us our debts,*
> *as we forgive our debtors.*

> *And lead us not into temptation,*
> *but deliver us from evil:*
> *For thine is the kingdom, and the power,*
> *and the glory, for ever. Amen*
> Matthew 6:9b-13

That prayer was repeated three times. And the third time, as the words of the prayer were proceeding from my mouth, it was as though my entire being was praying. After the prayer was spoken the third time, the pressure left my head; the fire moved from the border of the ceiling, following its path back to the shade and vanished. In that moment, time stood still. Peace enveloped me, and I knew that the God Who answers by fire was alive and Jesus was His Son. I asked the Lord one more thing that evening. I asked him to please let Shelly know the truth—for without him I am nothing. I then fell into a deep, peaceful sleep.

When I awoke the following morning, I helped the children wash and dress for camp. As I was preparing breakfast, Shelly walked into the kitchen. I looked up at him and cautiously said that what Paul had told us was true. I told him that I had called out to God in the middle of the night and He had answered me. I tried to explain in detail what had happened. Shelly pointed his finger toward me and told me to take two aspirins, go back to bed and when I woke up, I would come back to my senses. That was Thursday morning and the following Sunday, Paul came to our home.

I was in the kitchen with my friend, Nancy, and Shelly's mother, along with my brother's wife, Elaine, when Paul walked into the room. In the presence of these Jewish ladies, I told Paul everything that had happened to me. He then told me that the prayer spoken was the only prayer that Jesus had ever taught. He explained that when one of His disciples asked, "Lord, teach us to pray," Jesus answered, "When you pray you say..." Paul repeated the prayer and I began to weep.

I realized then that it was Jesus who had touched me. It was Jesus who had come into my heart and cleansed everything within me. It was Jesus who had spoken those words through my mouth. When I called out, "Father, if You can hear me please answer me...," I thought it was the Father who had come to me. I did not know the Scriptures then as I do now that "no man cometh to the Father, but by Me." Paul was amazed with all that had taken place in my life. He gave me a Bible and a short while later returned to California.

My hunger to read the Scriptures was insatiable. It was difficult for me to understand how the rabbis could read the same writings and not see Jesus. In the *Torah* (The five books of Moses: Genesis, Exodus, Leviticus, Numbers and Deuteronomy), I saw Jesus. When I read the prophets, I could see they were writing of His coming, of His bringing salvation to our people and giving them a new heart. I began to wonder if perhaps the Bible Paul had given me did not contain the same writings as the rabbis read.

I asked Scottie to bring home a *Chumash* from the synagogue, so I could compare the writings for myself. (The *Chumash* is a book made up of *Torah,* the prophetic writings along with rabbinic commentaries and, the *Megillot,* which are the books of Ruth, Esther, Ecclesiastes and Song of Solomon.) What if I was involved with another god, not the God of Israel? What if the fire was strange fire? I became frightened. I was determined that reading the *Torah* and the prophets in the *Chumash* would reveal the Truth to me.

As I began to compare the *Chumash* with the Bible Paul had given to me, I wept. The English translation of *Torah* and the prophets and the Bible given to me were virtually identical. I remember when I read Verse 26, in Chapter I of Genesis: *And God said, "Let us make man in **our** image, after **our** likeness,"* and realized that the Scriptures were identical in their translations, I fell prostrate before the Lord and prayed for a long while.

It overwhelmed me when I realized that the God of Israel had revealed Jesus to me as the Lord and that my people could not see Him while reading the Holy Writings. As a Jewess, it was difficult for me to conceive why God opened my eyes and heart to receive Jesus as the Holy One, our Messiah, the Son of God and the Savior of the world.

❧❦

The Lord desires to be in a personal relationship with you. As a father instructs his children, so the Lord desires to instruct you as His child. Don't be afraid.

Call Out To Him

They shall come with weeping,
and with supplications will I lead them:
I will cause them to walk by the rivers of waters
in a straight way, wherein they shall not stumble:
for I am a father to Israel,
and Ephraim is my firstborn.
Jeremiah 31: 9

THE BURDEN

... and the government shall be upon his shoulder...
Isaiah 9:6

S oon after I came to faith in Jesus, Shelly's mother was diagnosed
with a brain tumor. She underwent surgery at Yale New Haven
Hospital, and it was a heartbreaking moment when the surgeon
told us the tumor was malignant. He removed as much as he could
without leaving her fully paralyzed. In order to prolong her life, he
suggested chemotherapy treatments with the hope of shrinking the
tumor. When Mom was able to leave the hospital, she and Dad came
to our home for a time of recuperation. Her right leg was paralyzed
and she did not have full use of her right arm or hand. The battle she
faced was overwhelming.

The sense of loss I felt in my heart for her, as well as my own
personal loneliness, caused a deep struggle in my soul. Because of
my faith in Jesus, Shelly and I were struggling in our marriage. My
parents and members of my family, as well as most of my friends,
thought I had lost my mind. The only believers I knew lived in
California, and it was difficult for me to discuss my struggles with
them over the phone. Every time I felt as though I could not go on
any longer, Mom's physical condition would turn critical, prompting
Paul to come from the West Coast to be with her. Our times together
were life-giving to me.

During one of my times of conflict, Shelly phoned to tell me that
Paul had arrived in New York. Shelly was driving to the city for a
business meeting and asked if I would like to join him and see Paul.

I had desired to speak with Paul face-to-face, and I remember being excited deep within my heart as we drove to Wall Street.

When we arrived, Shelly hugged Paul and proceeded on to his business meeting. As Paul and I walked down the narrow streets, he put his arm around me not speaking a word. I felt he sensed my deep wrestling and after a few moments of silence, Paul spoke in his soft, gentle voice, "June, you cannot save anyone. You cannot save Shelly or your children. Only Jesus saves. You have taken a burden upon yourself that belongs to the Lord alone. The Word of God says the government shall be upon his shoulder. The burden is too heavy for you to carry. The Lord desires to carry it for you. However, He will not take it from you. You need to give it to Him."

I was so thankful for Paul's words of wisdom. I felt as though the Lord Himself held me in His arms and comforted me, while Paul and I walked and talked.

In my bedroom that evening, I fell on my face before the Lord, "Thank You, Lord, for speaking to me today. I do release Shelly, our children and all those dear to me into Your hands. Please, Lord, be merciful and reveal Yourself to each of them as You are, King of the Jews." In that very moment, the burden lifted from my heart.

∽෧ଵ

I learned a valuable lesson, one that changed my life forever. The Lord desired to take my burden and carry it for me, but first I needed to release it to Him. The Holy Writings instruct us in the way we should go and when we obey, we will experience His life to overcome.

The Lord Is The Burden Bearer

Cast thy burden upon the LORD, and he shall sustain thee:
he shall never suffer the righteous to be moved.
Psalm 55:22

GAS SHORTAGE

And I heard a voice from heaven, as the voice of many waters…
Revelation 14:2a

Shelly's parents were still living at our home. Dad employed a nurse's aide five days a week to help bathe and dress Mom. The nurse's aide also drove Mom for her chemotherapy treatments at Yale New Haven Hospital.

Mom and I had very precious moments together sharing the Scriptures. We read from the book of Psalms and had discussions about the Messianic prophecies. We read from the prophets, and Mom would ask questions about what I believed they revealed concerning the coming of Messiah.

I recall one conversation we had in the den after reading Isaiah Chapter 53. I had asked her to whom Isaiah was referring. She replied, "Jesus of course! But remember, June, I was born a Jew and I will die a Jew." I was surprised at her response and I challenged her with something like: "Mom, remember Jesus was a Jew and He died for our sins as King of the Jews." My statement ended our conversation.

Shelly's parents had lived with us for several months when Norman and Rita offered to come to our aide, by staying at our home for a weekend. We decided that we would go to New York to visit my brother, Robert, and his wife, Elaine. We had missed being with them and we knew that we could rest in their apartment.

That was the fall of 1973, and there was a gas shortage in the United States. Many cars had bumper stickers that read, *Down with Israel—Give Us the Oil.* There were limits to the amount of gas sold to each customer. Norman and Rita arrived at our home late Friday afternoon. They informed me that all the gas stations on the parkway were closed. At that time, we owned a new Buick Electra that used about three-quarters of a tank of gas to get to New York. Because our gas gauge registered less than a quarter of a tank, I decided to go to the nearest station to make an appeal to an attendant to fill our tank.

When I arrived at the station, it was closed. I was discouraged because I thought we would not be able to get to my brother's house that evening. Then I remembered there were three gas stations near each other down the highway, close to New Haven. I thought that at least one of the stations would be open, since it was not yet five o'clock. I made a U-turn and headed toward New Haven.

As I drove past the road that I would have turned on to get to our home, I heard a voice that sounded like many waters speak these words, "Go home, My child." Perplexed, I asked, "Was that You, Lord?" I heard the same audible voice repeat, "Go home, My child." I thought, "Lord, You know that I need gas. That could not have been You speaking." I continued driving toward New Haven ignoring the words of the voice I had just heard.

When I reached my destination, all three stations were closed, so I turned the car around to return home. I was distraught, not because I had not been able to fill up our tank with gas, but rather because I had disobeyed the One telling me to go home. I began to weep. I drove to the side of the road to park and prayed, "Lord, You know that I knew it was You who spoke. You tried to help me and I ignored Your voice. Can You please forgive me for not obeying You?" I wept bitterly. I heard again, the still small gentle voice say, "It's alright, My child, go home." As I drove home, peace filled my heart and the fragrance of the Lord filled the car.

Shelly was waiting for me, and I explained to him what had just taken place. I asked if we could attempt driving to New York that evening and trust the Lord to provide the gas. I was surprised when he agreed. As we drove out of our driveway, we knew we did not have enough gas to complete our journey. There was anticipation for what the Lord might accomplish through this apparent impossible circumstance, and it filled my heart with hope.

As we drove past the first gas station on the highway, Shelly turned to me and said, "There is someone sitting in the office at that station." The gas station was closed; nevertheless, I asked Shelly if he would consider backing up into the station and if he would allow me to ask the man for assistance. I was surprised when he backed up into the station responding, "Sure, June, you can go and ask him to help us." I knocked on the door of the office, and the young man welcomed me inside. I asked him if he would help us. I told him about our difficult situation at home. We now had the opportunity to rest in New York City, but we did not have enough gas to get there. To my relief and great surprise, the young man smiled and told me that it was not a problem. He would love to help us.

I followed him to the gas pump and watched the young man jump for joy, as he observed the monitor registering the gas. He chuckled as he filled our tank to the brim and exclaimed joyfully, "I have not seen this much gasoline going into one tank for months. I feel encouraged pumping this gas and filling up your tank." We could not thank the young man enough for his generosity and sensitivity to our situation.

That evening, as I pondered the events of the day, I thanked the Lord for His faithfulness even when I did not obey His voice. His concern for each detail of my life broke my heart and caused me to pray, "Lord, teach me to be faithful to You."

❧❧

Are you aware of God's concern for you in the every day circumstances of your life? His love and care is more than you could ever comprehend. Trust Him to make a way where there seems to be no way. As the Lord showed Himself faithful during the gas shortage, He desires to show Himself faithful to you in your time of need.

Lord, Teach Us To Trust And Obey

Call unto me, and I will answer thee,
and show thee great and mighty things,
which thou knowest not.
Jeremiah 33:3

A TENTATIVE WARDROBE

... I being in the way, the LORD led me...
Genesis 24:27

Paul was planning to be married in California during August of 1974. Shelly's parents had moved back to their home in Brooklyn, but they were still coming to Yale New Haven Hospital for Mom's chemotherapy treatments.

When Mom learned of the marriage plans, her desire was for a rabbi to perform the ceremony by her bedside. Paul took her request seriously and fasted and prayed about it. He received his answer from Jesus' own words, in Matthew 22:21:

Render therefore unto Caesar the things which are Caesar's,
and unto God the things that are God's.

That admonishment is written three times in the New Testament. Paul, therefore, believed he should take his marriage vows in the Name of Jesus; which a rabbi could not administer.

Shelly was mortified with Paul's decision and could not understand his reasoning. Yet, he would ask me over and over again, "What do you think about going to Paul's wedding?" Though my heart's desire was to attend the wedding, my reply was always the same, "If the Lord wants us to be there, He will make the way for us to go." My response to his question was inconsistent with my typical manner. I would usually have an opinion and readily communicate it. I must confess, my objectivity even surprised me.

One morning, my friend Claire, phoned. (Remember Claire who used to say I was glowing and asked if I were in love with Shelly?) She was very excited about a vacation she was planning to take in California. The airlines were offering a special fare from New York to California which included a rental car and hotel for four days and three nights. The entire vacation was available for what the airfare alone would normally cost. Although I doubted that Shelly would agree to attend Paul's wedding, I phoned him and told him about the special offer. He asked me to contact the airlines to make tentative reservations. He still had not come to a decision about going to the wedding.

I phoned my mother and asked if she would be able to take care of the children, if we went to California. I also went shopping and purchased a tentative wardrobe. I took my clothes to my dressmaker and asked if she could alter them by the following Thursday because our tentative flight reservations were for Friday.

The days that followed seemed to pass by quickly. It was Wednesday evening, and Shelly still had not come to a decision. To complicate matters, his father had phoned and urged him not to attend the wedding, not wanting Shelly to affirm Paul's faith in Jesus.

That night I had a dream. In my dream, Shelly was sitting by the foot of our bed with his back towards me. His elbows were on his knees as his hands supported his head. I was lying down on my pillow, and the space between us implied that we were not going to California. I asked him, "Have you come to your decision? Are we going to Paul's wedding?" Shelly answered emphatically, "Yes, we are going!" I was so surprised with his response that I tried to wake myself. As I was awakening, I heard the still small voice of the Lord say to me, "But you must abide by his decision."

My elbow was resting on Shelly's pillow and my chin was on my hand, as I stared into his sleeping face. He opened one eye and shut it quickly, and I was sure he had hoped he was dreaming. Finally, he opened his eyes and asked, "What are you doing up so early and why are you staring at me like that?"

I shared my dream with him and asked what he thought about it. He replied, "The first part of your dream could have been from the Lord, but the conclusion was your own desire. I have come to my decision about Paul's wedding. We are not going. Would you like to know the reason?" I told him I certainly would. He went on to say, "My father does not want us to attend Paul's wedding, and I feel I must honor his request."

I remembered the Lord's words to me that I must abide by his decision. I also realized that, although Shelly might not have known at the time, he was obeying a commandment to honor his father and his mother.

Later that morning, I went to the dressmaker to get my clothes. She asked me whether Shelly and I were going to California, and I told her that we were not going. She was a very expressive woman. She held up her hands, waving them up and down exclaiming, "I know you are going to California. You and your husband are beautiful people and you deserve to go. You are going to have the most wonderful time. You wait and see." I was stunned by her outburst.

I turned on the radio as I drove home and heard that the weather report was for cloudy skies and rain, yet the sun was shining brightly and there was not a cloud in the sky. At that moment, excitement began to well up within me about going to Paul's wedding. Why?

I turned into our driveway, parked and hurried into the house. I phoned Shelly and declared, "Your father's desire for us not to attend the wedding came from his personal feelings about Paul's faith. However, your mother's love for Paul is unconditional and although she has always honored your father, if she were well, she would be going to Paul's wedding." Shelly replied, "There is no way my mother would be going to Paul's wedding." I repeated, "Shelly, I know that if your mother was well, she would be going to Paul's wedding."

He responded, "June, I am going to meet my mother at the hospital this afternoon. She is coming for her chemotherapy treatment, and if she gives us her blessing to attend the wedding, we will go. Is that fair enough?" I responded, "That is fair enough."

As I hung up the phone, I heard the still small voice of the Lord say, "Go to the bank and get out the money. Go to the cleaners and get Shelly's clothes. Get out your suitcases and start packing. You are going to California."

As I was driving to the bank there were many thoughts racing through my mind. One thought was, "I could always redeposit the money if we did not go to California." After taking the money out of the bank, I drove to the cleaners to get Shelly's clothes. When I returned home I did bring our suitcases upstairs from the basement, though I must admit, I did not begin to pack. I waited and waited for Shelly to phone until – I could not wait any longer. I phoned him. His first words to me were, "Go to the bank and get out the money." I replied, "I already did."

ঔৰৰ্

Has the Lord promised something to you that seems impossible, or has He asked you to speak something that seems unreasonable? Listen for His voice and obey—the blessing will always follow.

God Still Speaks
Are You Listening For His Voice

Delight thyself also in the LORD;
and he shall give thee the desires of thine heart.
Commit thy way unto the LORD;
trust also in him;
and he shall bring it to pass.
Psalm 37:4, 5

A MOTHER'S BLESSING

... and do not forsake your mother's teaching.
Proverbs 6:20b

When Shelly arrived at the hospital, he decided not to talk to his mother unless he could do it privately. It appeared impossible to be alone with her, so he gave up trying. He walked into the nearest linen closet and banged his fist on the shelf saying, "You are not God! You could not even make a way for me to be alone with my mother."

As he turned to leave the closet, blocking the door was his mother in her wheel chair. Shelly was about to talk with her, but all he could say was, "Mom," because she began to cry. He asked her why she was crying and she responded, "I know what you are going to ask me. If I were well, I would be going to Paul's wedding. Shelly, go with June. You have my blessing."

As I began to pack our suitcases that evening, I was amazed. To think that Mom had spoken the same words to Shelly that I had spoken to him overwhelmed me. The Lord had put His desire for us to go to Paul's wedding into Mom's heart. When we drove the children to my parents' home on Friday morning, I thought, "O ye of little faith. Did you not believe that God would fulfill the promise He gave to you in the dream? You are now on your way with Shelly to Paul's wedding in California."

I somehow knew that God was going to move on Shelly's heart. When we arrived at the airport in California, there were young people handing out tracts about Jesus. In the parking lot were dozens of church buses. When we settled into our hotel room, we heard church

25

bells ringing and discovered that the church was directly across the street. Both Shelly and I were aware that God had ordained this time.

The evening we arrived, we visited with Phil and Joan, Paul's Jewish friends who had moved with him from Brooklyn. They had married after they received Jesus as their Messiah. Phil told us how he came to believe in Jesus and it had a profound affect on Shelly because he had known Phil for many years. It just was not like the Phil he remembered. Phil was always so logical, practical and very intelligent. How could this have happened to him? This faith he was proclaiming seemed so irrational. So absurd!

Joan was overseeing the food preparations for the reception. The pastor's wife had designed and made Adrienne's wedding dress. The women of the congregation had picked fresh flowers for the bridal bouquets. They also had arranged center pieces for the tables at the reception. Shelly realized that Paul's wedding was different from any he had ever attended. However, at that time he was not interested in Who made the difference.

The presence of the Lord was powerful at their ceremony. It was unlike anything Shelly or I had ever experienced. I was deeply touched when the doors of the church opened wide for the reception. Whosoever desired to come was welcome to dine with the bride and groom at their wedding feast. We were deeply affected by the love we experienced from the guests who attended.

The following morning, Paul and Adrienne departed for their honeymoon and we met them later on that evening at Big Sur. We have wonderful memories of our walks on the beach, as we were all more aware than ever of God's revealed glory in His creation.

Shelly and I continued on to Los Angeles the next morning. The views on Highway One were breathtaking. As we rounded each bend, it was as if we were turning the page of a book with each view being more magnificent than the one before. When we arrived in Los Angeles, the Dodgers were scheduled to play and much to my surprise, Shelly, an avid Dodger fan, chose rather to go to a healing service at a Christian Faith Center.

About 6,000 people attended that meeting. After the service we tried to speak with a man who purportedly was a former rabbi. Shelly had reasoned within himself that neither Paul nor I were still Jewish. How could we be? We believed in Jesus! But a rabbi, that was different. I explained our situation to his secretary and she conveyed the rabbi's response; he did not have the time to meet with us. I was deeply disappointed, however years later we discovered that the man had been a fraud. God had spared us.

After leaving the rabbi's office, we went to the bookstore to purchase his written material. As Shelly was thumbing through the rabbi's books, the Lord caught my attention with a book entitled *Ben Israel: Odyssey Of A Modern Jew* by Arthur Katz. I heard the still small voice of the Lord say, "Give this book to Shelly; it is for him." That is exactly what I did.

We decided to shorten our trip by one day. At that time, Shelly had a terrible fear of flying, so he had prayed what he describes as his first real prayer: "Lord, You know that I don't like to fly. I'm scared. If it is my time to die that is fine. But if it is the pilot's time, I don't want to go with him. If this is the right flight for us to take, I want June to say to me on the way to the airport tomorrow, 'Shelly, I know this is the right flight because it is such a beautiful day.' And, if You can do that, I also want You to put a celebrity on board the plane. Maybe then I will believe You are God."

On the way to the airport I remember looking up at the beauty of the heavens. The sky was so blue and the sun shone brighter that day than I had ever remembered. I was so moved that I turned to Shelly and said, "I know this is the right flight because it is such a beautiful day." I was not aware of his prayer at that time and he told me years later, that for a moment he had lost control of the car. Shelly found it hard to believe that God would care enough for him that He would answer his prayer by having me speak those exact words.

On the flight home, about midway across the country, Shelly looked around to locate a stewardess. He noticed they were all surrounding a man named Jack Edwards who was a host of a daytime television quiz show. There was his celebrity.

When we returned home, I noticed a genuine change in Shelly. For example, when the children were settled in for the night, I read my Bible in the den and Shelly would sit beside me reading *Ben Israel,* the book I had given him. The Lord was softening his heart, no doubt about it. Arthur had written about the hound of heaven being after him, and Shelly could identify. Arthur was a Jewish man born in Brooklyn, an intellectual who came to believe that Jesus is the God of Israel. "Unbelievable!" Shelly thought, "Was Art a traitor, or could it be true?" He desired to meet this Arthur Katz and speak with him in person.

Shelly's secretary, Catherine, was a born again Catholic believer who was praying for his salvation. She had heard that Arthur Katz was scheduled to be the next guest speaker at The Full Gospel Businessmen's breakfast meeting in New Haven, so she asked Shelly if he would like to hear Arthur speak. Shelly told her that he had desired to meet Art face-to-face and asked Catherine to please purchase two tickets for the breakfast, which she did.

∽૭૨ৈ∾

Thank You, Lord, that You are willing and able to change the heart of man. Thank You, Lord, that You are able to speak Your words through men. Thank You, Lord, that You enable us to know Your will. Thank You, Lord, for answering the prayers of those who earnestly seek You. Thank you, Lord, You do communicate with us in many different ways.

And I Thank You, Mom, For Releasing Shelly To God By Giving:

A Mother's Blessing

He will receive blessing from the LORD
and vindication from God his Savior.
Psalm 24:5

PAUL'S LETTER

Like cold water to a weary soul is good news from a distant land.
Proverbs 25:25

Shelly had finished reading the book, *Ben Israel*. His secretary, Catherine, had given him a tape of Arthur Katz's testimony which I listened to while I was driving home one afternoon. Before entering our driveway, I stopped to check our mailbox where I discovered a letter from Paul. In his letter, written in large bold print was: Arthur Katz, Belvedere Road, Plainfield, New Jersey, with his telephone number. Paul did not know that Shelly had read Arthur's book, nor was he aware that we had tickets to hear him speak in New Haven. My hands began to shake as my heart pounded hard and fast. I realized that God was moving mightily on our behalf.

I was so excited that I ran into our home, leaving our car in the driveway with the motor still running. How did Paul know Arthur? How did he get his address? Why was he giving us his telephone number? All these questions raced through my mind as I hurried to the phone to call Paul.

My heart was still pounding as I dialed his number. Paul was surprised to hear my voice. I asked him all the questions that were racing through my mind. Arthur had been a guest speaker at Paul's church, and Paul had told Arthur about us. Because he was scheduled to speak in New Haven, he gave Paul his address and phone number to pass on to Shelly. Arthur told Paul that he would look forward to meeting with us during his days in Connecticut.

Paul went on to say that when Arthur had originally received the invitation to speak in New Haven, his calendar was filled for those dates. He informed the president of the chapter that he was unavailable to accept the invitation. However, whenever Arthur approached his desk, the invitation from the New Haven chapter would be staring him in the face. He could not understand how that was possible since he kept throwing it into his wastepaper basket.

Suddenly, the meetings Arthur originally had scheduled for November were canceled. He then phoned the president of the Full Gospel chapter and informed him that he would be able to be their speaker, if those dates were still available. The president was delighted.

I could hardly believe what I was hearing. When I explained to Paul that we had purchased Arthur's book in Los Angeles and we had tickets for his meeting, Paul was in awe of all that had taken place. He asked me to please stay in close touch with him.

After I hung up, I ran outside to park our car in the garage. I was too excited to wait until Shelly came home to tell him the news, so I phoned him at the office. He was surprised to hear that Paul had met Arthur and he asked me for his telephone number, desperately desiring to talk directly with him.

About twenty minutes passed when Shelly phoned sounding bewildered. Arthur's first words to him when he called were, "Hello, brother!" Shelly could not understand why he would greet him as brother, since he had never even met the man. To add to Shelly's frustration, he had intended to ask Art if he could speak with him after the meeting. Instead, he heard himself asking, "Art, how would you and your family like to spend the weekend with us at our home when you come to New Haven?" Art replied, "We would love to." Shelly said that he felt like a fisherman who wanted to reel his words back into his mouth, but it was too late. Arthur Katz and his family were to be our house guests for the weekend.

The timing of Art's visit was very interesting because a number of months prior to Shelly's conversation with Arthur, the Lord had requested that I give Him our home. My initial thought at that time was that our closets were so messed up that our house was not clean enough for the Lord. As a result of that encounter, I had diligently worked to clean and organize all of our closets, even the ones in the basement. Our home was now prepared for the King of Glory to come in.

I had no idea at that time that the Lord would actually be visiting with us as a guest in our home through the life of one of His servants. In my wildest dreams, I never could have imagined that in the very near future, the Lord would reveal Himself to Shelly and call him by name, bidding Shelly to come and labor with Him in His vineyard.

⋙⋘

Are you praying for a loved one who appears to be far from God? Remember, Shelly thought I was crazy. Remember, I gave Shelly to the Lord. Remember how the Lord faithfully hounded him. God intervened! Keep praying for your loved one and never stop until …

The Spirit Of The Living God Moves On Your Behalf

May the LORD fulfill all your petitions.
Now I know that the LORD saves His anointed;
He will answer him from His holy heaven,
With the saving strength of His right hand.
Save, O LORD;
May the King answer us in the day we call.
Psalm 20:5b, 6, 9

ART'S VISIT

WHO HAS believed our message
and to whom has the arm of the LORD been revealed?
Isaiah 53:1

A rt with his wife Inger and their three children were approaching the driveway of our home—*is anything too difficult for the LORD?* Shelly had not known what to expect, but he could never have imagined Art's first words. As Art stepped out of his car, he looked at Shelly and asked him if he had a ping-pong table. Shelly had prepared himself to defend his Jewishness, but instead, he was asked to defend his ping-pong abilities. What could he think but, "*Oy vey,* I am in trouble."

After dinner, our Jewish friend, Donnie, came to visit and joined Shelly and Art in the dining room. Donnie intended to support Shelly in his conviction about being Jewish. While loading the dishwasher, I listened to their conversation and thought, "Lord, You have sent Your servant to our home to relieve me of my burden. Thank You, Lord. Arthur does not sound like any Jew I have ever met. What sort of man is he?"

Later on that evening, my parents along with my nephew, Jack, arrived for the weekend. My parents were going to be taking care of the children while we attended the breakfast meeting. In the morning, I was deeply moved when I saw Arthur on his knees by the window in our den.

When we arrived at the banquet hall of the hotel, Art asked the president of the chapter if Shelly and I could sit at the dais table with him and Inger, which we did. However, Shelly was extremely uncomfortable facing 600 people. He thought they were all staring at him. He whispered, asking me why they looked so happy, he could not understand why they were all smiling since it was so early in the morning.

As for me, well, I was in awe of the ways of God. I could never have imagined in my wildest dreams that Shelly and I would ever be sitting at the dais table of a Christian banquet, next to a Jewish speaker, who was a guest in our home with his family.

After breakfast, Art shared his testimony. Shelly, having read his book, did not appear moved by what he heard. At the conclusion of his message, Art asked, "Where are the Pauls and Silases of this city? Where are the Jews who will trouble their cities? Where are the men and women who are not looking for B'nai Brith (a Jewish charitable organization) awards? Where are the men and women who are not looking to be the citizen of the year or receive their recognition from men? Where are the men and women who will take the rewards of Paul and Silas, thirty-nine stripes on their back, imprisonment and ultimate death? Does anyone present desire to be like Paul and Silas? If so, stand to your feet."

I was amazed at how many people were moved to tears and standing. Shelly later shared his thoughts with me, "Since Art was our house guest, I thought I should at least stand and add credence to what he was saying. But, who in the world are Paul and Silas?"

As he was thinking those thoughts, the Holy Spirit kicked his chair out from under him. Suddenly, he was standing to his feet to be like Paul and Silas. He stood plastered against the wall behind him and I stood to join with Shelly for all the Lord had planned for us to do. I wept.

At the conclusion of the meeting, men and women were embracing Shelly saying, "Praise the Lord!" and "Isn't God good?" Shelly was wondering why they were so excited since he did not know the Lord or if He was good. What was wrong with these people? Shelly stood to a call to be like a Paul or Silas and he did not even know Jesus.

Before Arthur spoke at the evening meeting, I was asked to share my testimony. My parents were present since we were able to get a baby-sitter for the children. It was the first time that they heard how I came to believe in Jesus. Arthur spoke about Paul and Silas from the text of Acts 16. After the meeting, we decided to go directly home because we were all exhausted from the activities of that day.

When we arrived home, I prepared coffee and was slicing the cake to serve as Arthur walked into the kitchen with my father and Shelly. They appeared to be enjoying their evening snack when Arthur turned to my father and asked, "Gus, why is it that Isaiah 53 is not read in the synagogues today? What is it about that portion of Scripture? Why is it, Gus, that Isaiah 51 is read one week, and then Isaiah 52 is read the next week, then Isaiah 54 the following week?"

Shelly appeared to be more affected by the questions than my father. I had read him Isaiah 53 countless times. Arthur then asked my father if he wanted to hear Isaiah 53, and my father agreed to listen. As Arthur began to read to my father, Shelly had a sovereign revelation. Arthur read:

WHO HAS believed our message and to whom has the arm of the LORD been revealed?

He was despised and rejected by men, a man of sorrows, and familiar with suffering. Like one from whom men hide their faces he was despised, and we esteemed him not.

Surely he took up our infirmities and carried our sorrows, yet we considered him stricken by God, smitten by him, and afflicted.

But he was pierced for our transgressions, he was crushed for our iniquities; the punishment that brought us peace was upon him, and by his wounds we are healed.

We all, like sheep, have gone astray, each of us has turned to his own way; and the LORD has laid on him the iniquity of us all. He was oppressed and afflicted, yet he did not open his mouth;

he was led like a lamb to the slaughter, and as a sheep before her shearers is silent, so he did not open his mouth.

Yet it was the LORD's will to crush him and cause him to suffer, and though the LORD makes his life a guilt offering, he will see his offspring and prolong his days, and the will of the LORD will prosper in his hand.

After the suffering of his soul, he will see the light of life and be satisfied; by his knowledge my righteous servant will justify many, and he will bear their iniquities.
Isaiah 53:1,3,4,5,6,7,10,11

It was then that Shelly's mind and heart were enlightened by the Holy Spirit of God to understand for the first time that Isaiah was speaking of the Messiah. Several weeks later, Shelly shared these thoughts with me that he had at that time: "Lord, I think you have me, but I will give You one last chance to prove Yourself. If I can be alone in the car with Art tomorrow, I will know that You, Jesus, are the Holy One of Israel and I will give You my life and serve You with all my heart."

We were all scheduled to go to church the following morning. Our families together totaled ten. Shelly's thinking was that with ten people, eight would not ride in one car and two in the other. There was no way that he could be alone with Art in the morning. So he thought!

Sunday morning, Shelly seemed different. He did not speak a word to me although he appeared to be deeply moved. I explained to him why I could not go to church that morning. We had invited about eighty people to our home for an afternoon meeting to hear Art speak, and I needed the time to prepare food platters and to straighten up the house.

Shelly seemed to be in a daze as he walked to the front door. He stood with one hand on his waist staring out into space when Arthur grabbed him by the arm and said to him, "Come on, Shel. Inger is not ready. She will join us later. We are going to church alone in your car." Shelly explained to Art how the Lord had answered his prayer as they sat together, alone in our car. Arthur led Shelly in a prayer of salvation and officially welcomed him into the kingdom of God. The next time I saw Shelly, he was a new man.

All our Jewish neighbors and friends who were at our home that afternoon had a memorable experience. They had never before heard a Jewish man speaking with such authority about Jesus being the Messiah. This was their first encounter hearing about Jesus being the God of Israel, The Promised One. That Sunday afternoon meeting was an event, sealed up and recorded in heaven.

On Sunday evening, Arthur was asked to remain one more day. What a difference a day makes. He was to speak to the divinity students at Yale. Monday morning, after Shelly went to work, Pastor Andrews phoned and wanted to speak with Arthur. He paused from their conversation for a moment to ask me if I had ever been baptized. I said I was waiting for Shelly to come to the Lord because I desired to be baptized with him. Arthur's next words to Pastor Andrews were, "Fill up the tank."

After he hung up the phone, I asked him why he told Pastor Andrews to fill up the tank. Shelly was not ready to be baptized. Arthur said that he would take care of Shelly, since he was meeting him at Yale Divinity School and would speak with him about being baptized. Arthur told me to wear old clothes and to have Shelly's clothes ready as well as several towels.

Shelly arrived home late that Monday afternoon. I had his clothes and the towels folded together on the kitchen table. He walked directly to the refrigerator and began to chew on a piece of chicken. He said that Art wanted us to meet him at church to see a baptism. I swallowed hard and asked if that was all Art had said to him? He answered, "Yes, why?" I asked slowly and suspiciously, "Did he tell you whose baptism it was?" Shelly glanced at me with a funny look on his face and answered, "No, why?"

I pointed my finger at him and declared, "It's yours!" He responded firmly, "Oh, no, it's not! I just accepted Jesus and I'm not getting baptized." I asked if I could take his clothes and the towels to the church, just in case he changed his mind. He said that I could, although he told me explicitly to walk directly to the back pew, sit down and not say a word.

We arrived at the church as Arthur was giving instructions to those who were getting baptized. When he finished speaking, he began walking up the aisle toward us. Shelly was moving lower and lower into his seat. Art looked at him asking, "*Nu*! (So!) Why aren't you going with the men to change your clothes?" Shelly said he was not getting baptized because he had put out a fleece to the Lord, and the Lord did not answer it. He again told Arthur that he was not getting baptized. Arthur replied in a tone that is uniquely Art, "Oh really! When the Scriptures tell us, *Whoever believes and is baptized shall be saved...* Shel, you do not question God about something that is clearly written in His Word." Shelly repeated resolutely to Art that he was not getting baptized.

About twenty minutes later, Arthur lifted me up from the waters of baptism. Truly, it was a miracle, because I was touched anew by the hand of God. He then lifted Shelly up from the waters of baptism. How did that happen? God was in charge! There we were in the water, three Jews who knew that Jesus was the Messiah, embracing in the baptismal pool in a Baptist Church while a born-again Catholic nun, Sister Charlotte, was singing the Alleluia chorus. Shelly thought he was in heaven. God's ways are past finding out.

After the baptisms, Arthur served us the Lord's Supper and Shelly's face was radiant. It was the first time he had received the bread and the wine as a remembrance of Jesus' death until He returns.

In the Lord's faithfulness to Israel, communion has been hidden in the partaking of the *Oneg Shabbat,* which is the breaking of bread and drinking of wine. This tradition is celebrated in synagogues throughout the world after their Sabbath service.

That evening, the president of the Full Gospel Businessmen's chapter gave each of us a Bible. Later on that evening, Scott and Dean asked if they could each have a personal Bible. At that time, they did not know that their father had acknowledged Jesus, nor were they aware that we had just been baptized. Shelly gave Scott his new Bible and I gave Dean mine, and Arthur wrote a dedication for the boys in their new Bibles. That evening, I experienced the fulfillment of God's promise in His Word from the book of Acts, Chapter 16 and Verse 31.

❦❦

Keep praying and believing until that evening arrives in your life and in the life of your loved one. You will say and believe…

The Lord Is My Light And My Salvation

They replied,
"Believe in the Lord Jesus, and you will be saved—
you and your household."
Acts 16:31

THE FIRST THANKSGIVING

Whoever acknowledges me before men,
I will also acknowledge him before my Father in heaven.
Matthew 10:32

My mother-in-law's physical condition was failing, and it seemed best for her to move to New Jersey to live with Norman and Rita. They built an additional bedroom and bathroom onto the lower level of their home. My father-in-law employed a full-time nurse's aide to help care for Mom.

Norman and Rita invited us to celebrate Thanksgiving with them in their home. Shelly was concerned about how his mother would receive the news of his new found faith in Jesus. His anxiety level seemed to rise as we approached New Jersey. He struggled because he did not want to increase the grief that his mother was already experiencing. I tried to comfort Shelly by reassuring him that the Lord was mindful of his concerns and would prepare the way before him. However, I never did expect the event that follows.

When we arrived, we were all so happy to be together that the tension in Shelly appeared to be relieved. The children were excited to be with their cousins, and it was always a special treat to be with their Grandma Lily and Grandpa Sol.

Rita was busy in the kitchen, so I joined her to help with the last minute preparations. Mom and Dad were occupied with the children when Norman and Shelly walked into the kitchen. Shelly took that opportunity to tell them that he believed that Jesus was the Messiah. They both appeared upset as Rita repeated several times,

"You, Shelly, you believe? How could you believe such a thing? You really believe?"

His faith in Jesus shook up the entire family, one-by-one. You can be sure of it. He was so conservative, so level-headed. Never would Shelly give himself to anything just because someone else had. He was a leader, not a follower, until he came to Jesus. Now Shelly followed the One our people desperately try to ignore. Rita was terribly shaken up over the news. No doubt about it.

It was time to serve the Thanksgiving meal. Rita attempted to compose herself before calling everyone to the dining room table. During the meal, Norman and Rita acted as though nothing unusual had taken place. We had a relaxed time as we reminisced and laughed together. It was soon time to serve the dessert. When the children had finished eating their meal, they asked to be excused to play outside. Norman was helping Rita clear the table and load the dishwasher in the kitchen. Before we knew it, everyone had left the dining room except Shelly, Mom and me.

We were sitting at the head of the table while Mom sat in her wheelchair at the foot. She lifted her arm and pointed her finger toward Shelly and said calmly, "You are just like Paul now, aren't you?" We were stunned by Mom's perception. A bit shaken up, Shelly asked his mother how she knew that he was just like Paul. In her gentle loving way, she responded, "I can see it in your eyes, Shel. There is a peace that was not there before. You have not been able to look directly at me since I have been ill, until today."

Shelly walked over to Mom, fell to his knees and embraced her. She did not appear upset with his new found faith in Jesus. She knew deep within her heart that the change in Shelly was good. Somehow, her faith in God had opened her eyes to see. Mom never did speak with him again about his belief.

On one other occasion, Shelly had the opportunity to be alone with Mom, but by that time she had lost her capacity to speak. Although she was unable to verbally communicate, we knew she understood everything that was being spoken. Shelly shared the gospel with her and asked her to blink her eyes once if she believed

Jesus was the Lord, and twice if she did not believe. Instantly, she blinked once. Shelly prayed for Mom as she gave her heart to Jesus as the Promised One, the Messiah and the Holy One of Israel.

Before Mom lost her ability to speak, she had said to me that she was born a Jew and she would die a Jew, and so she did. She took her last breath on earth knowing the King of the Jews.

Mom went home to be with the Lord, the One she revered and loved for so many years, without even knowing His Name. Now she knows His Name is *Yeshua,* Jesus. She is beholding His face in the world to come. It is truly comforting to know that our children will once again see their beloved Grandma Lily. I know she looks forward to the day when she will hold them in her arms once again.

That first Thanksgiving was more significant than we could ever have imagined. The Lord proved Himself to be faithful and trustworthy. The Scriptures tell us that the eye is the window of our heart. The Lord enlightened Mom's heart to see the faith of God in Shelly's eyes. She understood how his new found faith allowed him to trust God and freed him to accept her illness. Shelly's faith enabled his heart to be opened to Mom without fear. And so he did. And my faith in Jesus was strengthened by this testimony.

∽୧౷∾

Trust the Lord to enable you to share your faith in Jesus with your loved ones. Ask Him to give you the perfect opportunity. And, don't be surprised if your loved one asks you questions before you are able to say a word.

All Things Are Possible—Only Believe

Trust in the LORD with all your heart
and lean not on your own understanding...
Proverbs 3:5

THE FIRST PASSOVER SEDER

And when they were filled, He said to His disciples,
"Gather up the leftover fragments that nothing may be lost."
And so they gathered them up, and filled twelve baskets with
Fragments from the five barley loaves,
which were left over by those who had eaten.
John 6:12, 13

It was several months after Shelly became a believer that we started attending services at the Baptist Church where Arthur had baptized us. The time of Passover was drawing near when Pastor Andrews asked Shelly if he would conduct a *Seder* service. He said, "I would love to and I will have June cook the meal for the *Seder.*"

When Shelly told me about his discussion with Pastor Andrews, I asked him how many people were expected. When he told me that he had no idea, I felt a bit nervous because I didn't know how much food to prepare.

I retreated to our bedroom and took my familiar position on my knees by the window. I asked the Lord for help because this task seemed too overwhelming for me. Where do I begin? As I prayed, a deep peace filled my heart. I felt an assurance from the Lord that He would take care of everything.

As I observed Shelly researching the *Seder* service with all its hidden meaning, the Holy One seemed to be beckoning him to the Scriptures. Growing up in an orthodox home, where his father had conducted the *Seder* every year for the entire family, it could only have been divine revelation that brought Shelly beyond his Jewish traditions. There seemed to be new enthusiasm within him, and it excited me to watch Shelly spending time with Scott and Dean, explaining to them his revelation of Jesus as the Messiah. A greater burden was birthed in our hearts to pray that the Lord would open the eyes of our people.

When I arrived at the church kitchen, with all the groceries I had purchased for the *Seder* meal, I was surprised to see women waiting to help me prepare the food. The menu was to be: *Gefilte Fish* on a Bed of Lettuce, *Matzah Ball Soup*, Turkey with Passover Stuffing, Sweet Potatoes, *Kugel,* String Beans Almandine and Salad. Dessert was a sheet cake, baked by a good friend, Cathy.

We had our work cut out for us cooking the food, setting the tables and preparing and arranging the elements on the *Seder* service plates. We were setting 100 places, although we still were not certain how many guests would be attending. I must confess that the food I had brought to prepare for the *Seder* meal would feed only eighty people.

The ladies worked diligently all day with expectation for the meal and *Seder* service. After the preparations were completed, I went home to shower and change. It was not until then that I realized the privilege given to me, to be able to cook in God's house for His people and for one of His appointed feasts.

I returned to the church about an hour before the *Seder* service was to begin. I experienced the Lord's faithfulness once again. There was a couple who had catering experience, waiting to help carve the turkey, and they asked if they could help coordinate all the activities in the kitchen.

Shelly's secretary, Catherine, worked by my side. I stood on a chair to reach into the large pot to stir the *matzah ball* soup. (Remember, I am all of 4'11"!) I realized then that there were not enough *matzah balls* for 100 people. I remember being upset and saying, "Lord, You promised me there would be enough food for everyone."

Catherine and I found it hard to believe what happened next. For a split second, all we saw in that large pot of soup were *matzah balls*. Before our very eyes were hundreds of *matzah balls*! No soup! Then the soup covered the *matzah balls* just as if nothing unusual had taken place. Catherine was flabbergasted. She stared at me with her eyes wide open and with a shaky voice exclaimed, "If I had not seen that happen with my own eyes, I would never have believed it."

As we were arranging the *Seder* service plates, the gentleman pouring the wine came to tell me that there was only a tenth of the bottle left, and there were yet many more glasses to be filled. During the *Seder* service, wine is used to sip as well as to pour out for each of the ten plagues. I encouraged him to fill the glasses with wine until the bottle was empty. What else could we do at this late hour?

He returned about five minutes later with a bewildered look on his face. I repeated, "It's alright," seeing there was still about a tenth of wine remaining in the bottle. I tried to encourage him by saying, "Just pour the wine until the bottle is empty." He looked shaken as he explained, "I cannot believe what just happened. I poured the wine into the glasses and I poured and poured until all the glasses were filled and look, there is still the same amount of wine remaining."

The guests were arriving, and all the food was ready to be served. We had a dais table set where Shelly and I were to sit with Scott, Dean and Suzi, along with Pastor Andrews and his wife, Lydia. Ninety-eight people arrived and were seated. The *Seder* service was ready to begin.

Shelly stood up and said, "Jesus is our Messiah and Lord." That was the first time he had spoken *Hashem, Yeshua* (The Name, Jesus) publicly. He prayed and the *Seder* officially began. As he read from the Scriptures, you could feel the presence of the Lord. He completed the first part of the *Seder* service and it was time to serve the meal.

The couple with catering experience directed the women in the kitchen who were to serve the food. It was as though we had planned every detail. Only those serving knew it was the Lord's faithfulness and divine order at work in the kitchen.

I personally emptied the food out of every pot and used every tray from the oven to serve. Everyone seemed to love the meal as they were taking second and third helpings. What an inspiring experience to see the joy and celebration that was evident in the people at the *Seder.*

Dessert was about to be served. My friend, Cathy, who was cutting the cake, informed me that as much as she tried to get more than eighty slices from the sheet cake, it was not going to happen. I encouraged her to slice the cake and to serve it without concern.

She returned to the kitchen a short time later. "I was slicing and serving the cake, when people came back for a second piece. I did not see the cake increase, but I do know how many slices there should have been. I have served more than 100 pieces and as unbelievable as it sounds, we still have half a sheet cake remaining." We again experienced the Lord's faithfulness to His promise.

Now to Him who is able to do exceeding abundantly
beyond all that we ask or think,
according to the power that works within us.
Ephesians 3:20

The *Seder* service resumed. Shelly's face was radiant as he spoke. He lifted up the last element to be eaten, the piece of *matzah* that was hidden and then found by one of the children.

This piece of *matzah* is called *Afikomen.* Our people think it means dessert because it is the last thing eaten at the *Seder. Afikomen* is not a Hebrew word; it is derived from a Greek word that means, "I Came." The significance is noteworthy, since the next cup held up is the cup of Redemption. Shelly read from the Scripture about Jesus' celebration of the Passover:

And when He had given thanks, He broke it, and said,
"This is My body, which is for you;
do this in remembrance of Me."
In the same way He took the cup also,
after supper, saying,
"This cup is the new covenant in My blood;
do this, as often as you drink it,

in remembrance of Me."
I Corinthians 11:24 – 26

Jesus truly is our redemption and by His blood, which was shed at Calvary, we have forgiveness for our sins. The fourth and last cup is the cup of praise and Shelly lifted it up and prayed in Hebrew.

My heart was filled with deep gratitude to God once again as I realized that He had allowed me to recognize Jesus as the Lamb of God who takes away the sins of the world. We rejoiced with our guests in Hebraic worship and dance.

The couple with catering experience oversaw the details cleaning up. Pastor Andrews approached me and asked, "What do you want me to do with all the leftover food?" I smiled and answered, "You do not have to be concerned with leftovers, Pastor, I personally emptied all the pots and trays. All the food that we served was eaten."

With a surprised expression on his face he replied, "Oh, really? There is enough food remaining in the pots and on the trays in the oven to feed a nursing home."

That is just what happened. Pastor Andrews and his wife brought all the fragments to a nursing home, and there was enough food to feed all the residents. And, I believe the men and women who ate the leftovers of that Passover meal never tasted food quite so good in all their lives.

☙❧

Are you overwhelmed with a task that seems impossible for you to accomplish? Remember, God's fragments are far greater than our resources. Don't get frustrated—get excited. And, be ready to experience …

The Lord's Intervention

Jesus Christ is the same yesterday and today and forever.
Hebrews 13:8

THE FIRST YOM KIPPUR

Speak, LORD, for your servant is listening.
1 Samuel 3:9

The first *Yom Kippur* (The Day of Atonement), after Shelly came to know Jesus, we visited with a cell group of a German monastic order in New Jersey at the home they had purchased from Arthur Katz. We were asked to join with them in two hours of silence, as we fasted and prayed for our people.

Each of us was assigned a room along with Scripture verses to read. After reading the verses, we were instructed to invite the Father, Jesus and the Holy Spirit into the room. When we felt His presence, we were to thank Him for joining with us and ask Him if He had anything on His heart to speak. If He did speak, we were to write it down and when the two hours were completed, we would meet together to share what we had experienced.

As I sought to pray, both kneeling and lying on my bed felt awkward. I decided to sit on the rocking chair to read the verses. I invited the Father, Jesus and the Holy Spirit to come into the room and as I prayed, I felt chills cover me from the top of my head to the tip of my toes. I remember thinking, "Lord, was that really You? Lord, You may say to me, *"O ye of little faith."* However, if that was really You, could You please touch me one more time." Instantly, chills covered me again from the top of my head to the tip of my toes. I sobbed as I breathed in His presence. Peace unspeakable filled my soul and I thanked the Lord for the visitation. I then asked, "Lord, is there anything You desire to say to me?"

The words the Lord spoke that first *Yom Kippur* have encouraged me through many seasons of trials and testing. May these words be a comfort to you, as they have been to me:

Don't be afraid
Keep your eyes on Me
I will give you all the strength you need
I want to convert your heart completely to Me
Be still My child and learn My Ways
They are not your ways
Learn this and I will change your name
The conversion of Sarai to Sarah
This is My desire for you

When we met together, Shelly explained how uncomfortable he had felt when he was alone in his room, so much so, he fell asleep. That was how he spent the first hour and a half. When he awoke, he asked the Lord if there was anything He wanted to say to him. The Lord said:

I Have Not Called You To A New Career
But To A New Way Of Life

∽ઝૅ৯

May the Lord grant you the grace to embrace the words written above as an impartation for your life.

Give Us An Ear To Hear—
And A Heart To Obey

I will instruct you and teach you in the way you should go;
I will counsel you and watch over you.
Psalm 32:8

SUZI'S DANCING SCHOOL

But in your hearts set apart Christ as Lord.
Always be prepared to give an answer to everyone who asks you
to give the reason for the hope that you have.
But do this with gentleness and respect.
I Peter 3:15

When Suzi was four years old, we sent her for ballet lessons to the dancing school that all her little Jewish friends attended. We car-pooled the girls and when it was my turn to drive, I would drop them off and go to the nearest supermarket to do my weekly grocery shopping.

One week after my supermarket run, I returned to the dancing school with time to spare and decided to read my Bible sitting on the steps of the school. A woman from the adjoining building opened the door and invited me inside because it was too cold and windy to read on the steps. She said it was much warmer and more comfortable in the building. I thanked her for being so kind as I walked inside. I was surprised to discover that the adjoining building was a church.

The woman was busy vacuuming, so not wanting to disturb her, I found my way to one of the pews and sat down. As I was thanking the Lord for allowing me to be with Him in a church building during the week, I thought I heard His still small voice asking me to pray for His Spirit to come into the building.

I was surprised. I thought His Spirit was in every church building, and I communicated that to Him. But the Lord seemed persistent in asking me to pray for His Spirit to come into the building. I was unsure as to why He was asking me to pray in that way, yet I knew I needed to obey.

Therefore, I prayed and welcomed the Holy Spirit into the church.

After praying, I thought the Lord wanted me to ask the woman if she knew Him. I told the Lord that I did not want to disturb her, and it would be rude of me to ask her such a question. The Lord told me to go ask her if she knew Him.

Reluctantly, I walked to the front of the church and asked if she knew the Lord. She turned off the vacuum and seemed perplexed asking, "What did you say?" I repeated my question, "Do you know the Lord?"

She looked shocked and asked me my religion. I felt awkward about the position I was in but proceeded to tell her that I was Jewish. My response seemed to shock her even more. With her voice trembling and her body shaking, she exclaimed, "You are Jewish! You are Jewish and you are asking me if I know the Lord? Just today, I asked the Lord to give me a sign if we were really living in the last days. I cannot believe that you are Jewish and you know the Lord." She began mumbling under her breath, "Is this really happening?"

Three weeks later, it was again my turn to car-pool. As I took the girls into their classroom, a woman was running toward me asking where I had been. She said she had looked for me every week since we had spoken in the adjoining building. She had told her husband about me and shared with everyone in her church what had happened the day we met. I explained that I car-pooled and drove every third week.

She gave me a gift and asked me to please not open it until I was in my car. I thanked her for being so thoughtful. The package was very small and neatly wrapped and before opening her present, I decided to do my grocery shopping.

Returning from the supermarket, the still small voice spoke to me not to open the package and better yet, He told me to give it back. How could I do that? She seemed to be so excited about giving me the gift and I really did not want to hurt her.

I asked the Lord if I could just throw the package away since she would never know. He was firm once again telling me to give the package back. He also told me to give her this message: "There is no other book that is truth except the Bible, from Genesis to Revelation." I tried to reason with the Lord one more time, but He remained firm about giving the package back.

When I drove into the parking lot I saw her waiting in her car. I parked in the spot next to her, walked over and knocked on the window. She seemed so excited to see me and invited me into her car. I was very nervous when I explained how sad I felt, because I was not able to accept her gift. I was shaking and told her that the Lord wanted me to give it back to her. I told her that there is no other book that is truth except the Bible, from Genesis to Revelation.

Waving the gift at me, she asked if I knew what was in the package. Tears rolled down my cheeks, seeing how upset she was, as I told her that I did not know what the package held. She asked if I had ever heard of Joseph Smith. I had heard about Joseph Smith and the Mormon faith but did not know much about it, and I told her so. The package she had given me contained the Book of Mormon.

Becoming increasingly upset, she asked sarcastically if the Bible was the only book I ever read. I explained that I did read other books and she was curious to know what sort of books. I told her that I read books on the history of my people and also Christian books about faith. I enjoyed reading autobiographies about believers and how the Lord met them in everyday life.

She asked me for an example and I mentioned *The Hiding Place* by Corrie Ten Boom. She appeared to calm down some, and I apologized again for upsetting her. As I opened the car door, the children were coming out from their dancing class. We bid our farewells. My heart was at peace because our relationship seemed to be intact.

Several months later, I received a phone call from her. She invited me to speak to the ladies at her church about the book *The Hiding*

Place; they had all read it and wanted to meet me. Overwhelmed, I asked Shelly if I should go to the church of The Latter Day Saints to speak to the women. He believed it was providential, so I accepted her invitation.

After I hung up, I went to my bedroom and knelt by the window. I asked the Lord what was on His heart for me to share. I thought He told me to read the preface of the book. It contained ten lessons learned through Corrie Ten Boom's experiences, by the couple who assisted her in writing *The Hiding Place*:

Handling separation	Security in the midst of insecurity
Getting along with less	Forgiveness
How God can use weakness	Dealing with difficult people
Facing death	How to love your enemies
Overcoming evil with good	What to do when evil wins

I was to share with the women on those ten lessons learned. Little did I know at that time, the Lord was going to bring me through all ten of those lessons to reveal Himself to me as the Faithful One, in and through them all.

I phoned two of my friends to fast and pray with me for the meeting. Fran was a Jewish believer and Judy was the wife of a Baptist pastor. They asked to come with me and I rejoiced.

When we arrived at the church, the women greeted us warmly. I spoke about the ten lessons learned from the book then the women wanted to know how, as a Jewess, I came to believe in Jesus.

After sharing my testimony everyone was weeping, including me. Suddenly, a woman stood and cried out that she wanted to know Jesus the way I knew Him. Then, every woman in the room was standing, simultaneously saying that they wanted to know Jesus as their personal Lord and Savior.

Judy, Fran and I stood up holding hands as I led the women in a prayer of salvation. Joy and laughter filled the room and the angels rejoiced in heaven, as we all embraced with our faces aglow.

Judy, Fran and I skipped to our car as we rejoiced in the Lord for what He had done. The event that took place that evening, in the church of The Latter Day Saints, was beyond anything we could ever have asked, imagined or thought.

I never did see the women again; however, you can be sure that their little church was forever changed. Can you imagine thirty or forty women, from the church of The Latter Day Saints, praying for their loved ones to know Jesus as their personal Lord and Savior?

∽ॐ৵

Life is exciting as you learn to hear and obey His voice. The results of obedience will amaze you. It amazed me!

Try It And See

Everyone was amazed and gave praise to God.
They were filled with awe and said,
"We have seen remarkable things today."
Luke 5:26

SO WHAT'S YOUR POINT

"Behold, the days come," saith the LORD,
"that I will make a new covenant with the house of Israel,
and with the house of Judah..."
Jeremiah 31:31

Suzi attended an orthodox Hebrew pre-school three days a week. A written notice was sent home to inform parents that an adult Bible study was to begin one evening a week. Shelly and I decided to attend the study with our orthodox Jewish neighbors and three Jewish believers.

The study never got past the first three words of the *Torah*, *"Bereshit Bara Elohim"* (In the beginning God). There was so much the rabbi had to say about the meaning behind those three words. The only time we discussed other Scriptures was when one of the Jewish believers in the class asked a question.

One evening, the rabbi informed us that he would not be teaching our class the following week. Another rabbi would be leading the study, because he had a special meeting that he needed to attend, downstairs in the building.

At the next Bible study, there was electricity in the air, an anticipation of something about to happen. We were half way through the study when Shelly raised his hand. The rabbi acknowledged him and Shelly asked what Jeremiah meant in Chapter 31 and Verse 31 when he talked about a new covenant. He asked the rabbi what was the new covenant that The Holy One had promised?

The rabbi responded, "Years ago, we did not have the Scriptures. Now we have the Scriptures and that is the new covenant in

Jeremiah." Once again Shelly asked the rabbi, encouraging him to read Jeremiah 31:31: *"Behold, the days come," saith the LORD, "that I will make a new covenant with the house of Israel, and with the house of Judah..."*

And again, he asked the rabbi what he thought that meant. The rabbi repeated himself again by saying that years ago, we did not have the Scriptures, but now we have the Scriptures and that is the new covenant.

Being persistent, Shelly asked the same question, still encouraging the rabbi to look at what Jeremiah was saying about the new covenant. Shelly read that portion of Scripture for the third time and asked the rabbi what Jeremiah was saying and what did he mean by a new covenant? Appearing very frazzled and frustrated by the question, the rabbi responded:

"So what's your point? What's your point?" As he stood to his feet with his arms waving in the air, he cried out, "What's your point?"

Shelly stood to his feet and boldly responded that his point was that the new covenant is the Good News that *Yeshua*, Jesus, is the Messiah for our people. It was as though the trumpet had blown in heaven and the angels were standing and gazing in amazement.

Everyone in the classroom had stood to their feet at the same time. We gathered into different groups with a Jewish believer in each group. It is a sovereign moment when *Hasidic* Jewish men (Ultra Orthodox Sect waiting for the Messiah) hear about the new covenant in their own school. The Spirit of God was leading us as we all began to read Isaiah 53 simultaneously.

One wall in the classroom was made of glass so you could see into the room from the stairwell. At the very moment that awe and excitement filled the air, our rabbi had walked to the top of the stairwell. He was elated when he observed us all reading from the Scriptures with enthusiasm. After all, we were his students. Everyone was standing with their Bibles opened running down the page with our fingers, following every word.

The rabbi entered the classroom light-footed, heading toward Shelly and Fran who were talking with the teacher who led the study that evening. Fran had graduated from that Hebrew Day School with honors. Our rabbi excitedly said to the teacher that Fran was wonderful, and he told him that he had taught her everything she knew. He walked in and out of the classroom several times, letting the teacher know how he had trained Fran and encouraged the teacher to listen to her. That encounter lasted well beyond the usual hours of our Bible study.

The following week, our rabbi opened the study by informing us that he was the teacher and there would be no more questions. He also informed us that the following week his son, Yosi, would be coming from Brooklyn to speak with us. Everyone at the study was very somber. No one spoke. We just listened.

Yosi arrived at the study with several *Hasidic* young men from Brooklyn; it was intense. He was one of the leaders of the *Hasidic* Sect and led a *mitzvah*-wagon. (A vehicle that carried *Hasidic* Jewish evangelists, calling Jewish people back to observing the law.) He had studied the New Testament in order to disprove its validity. Yosi was a man of the Word who loved the Holy One, but he did not know His Name.

He spoke with our class for a long time and then turned his attention to Shelly and me. He explained to us that as Jews, we were linked together. I was surprised how close his teaching was to the kingdom of God. Yosi really had a zeal for God, but not according to knowledge. He encouraged us to keep the law by saying prayers and following tradition. He could not comprehend that one could not make them self righteous by their deeds.

When he finished speaking, I asked him if he believed in a judgment day. He assured me he did, and we would each stand before the Holy One to be judged.

I then asked him, "What if Jesus is the Holy One? What if we have found the Truth? What if Jesus is the Messiah, the Son of God and the Savior of the world? What if Jesus is LORD, the God of Israel?" He stared at me with his eyes wide open while he listened intently. "The Lord might understand why you are not accepting what we are telling you, however, what would you say to the Holy One on judgment day if He should ask you, 'Yosi, why did you not ask Me?'"

He stood to his feet visibly shaken, "You people are all alike. You are so frustrating to deal with. Every encounter I have with people like you ends up the same way." I watched him in amazement as he threw his arms up in the air in thorough disgust.

I sensed that the Lord loved him so much, that other Jewish believers had been prompted to ask him that very same question. That deeply touched my heart and what a challenge it must have presented to him. The Lord desired to answer Yosi and He was waiting for him to ask directly, "Could it be that Jesus is The Holy One of Israel? *Abba,* (Father) Is Jesus Your Son?"

As I write today, it is hard for me to believe that more than thirty years have passed since that encounter. Yosi is now a leading *Hasidic* rabbi in Israel. About ten years ago, when Shelly and I were visiting his hometown, we phoned him. He said that he did not remember us, but he extended an invitation to attend the special ceremony for his son's first haircut. He told Shelly that he would call him back with directions after he picked his mother up at the airport.

He never did phone us back. Perhaps he or his mother remembered that Bible study class when the heavens were shaken. We continue to remember Yosi and his family in our prayers. Shelly was a very young believer when we attended that Bible study class, but he was given divine boldness to speak from the Scriptures.

�❧

Share the Good News with Jewish people. Tell them that Jesus is their Messiah. They need to know the Truth. Do not fear, obey the Word that tells you to go to the Jew first and also to the Greek. God asks us to plant seeds wherever we are, and sometimes He asks us to water the seeds that have already been planted. God Himself promises to give the increase. The Lord sends others to reap the seed when the harvest is ready. May your life bear fruit for His kingdom.

Lord Send Me

How then shall they call upon Him
in whom they have not believed?
And how shall they believe in Him
whom they have not heard?
And how shall they hear without a preacher?
And how shall they preach unless they are sent?
Just as it is written,
"HOW BEAUTIFUL ARE THE FEET OF THOSE
WHO BRING GLAD TIDINGS OF GOOD THINGS!"
Romans 10:14, 15

THE CALL

He who loves father or mother more than Me is not
worthy of Me; And He who loves son or daughter
more than Me is not worthy of Me.
Matthew 10:37

In August of 1975, we visited Art and Inger in Laporte, Minnesota. Art had purchased a farm, on an Indian reservation that was located four hours north of Minneapolis, where he had started a community of believers.

Across the road from the farm was a camp called Dominion, where family convocations were held during the summer. Believers from all over the world attended those gatherings. During our visit, Shelly accompanied Art to a camp meeting, while I remained at the farmhouse with Inger.

The instructor was teaching from the book of Ephesians when he asked, "To whom are you practically bound to in your home town?" Shelly heard an audible voice say to him, "You and your family belong here in Minnesota with Art."

He turned quickly to see who was behind him, but no one was there. The instructor continued his teaching and again asked, "To whom are you practically bound to in your home town?" Shelly heard a louder voice shout to him, "No one!" He turned quickly to see who was behind him, but no one was there.

He was quite shaken and prayed, "Lord, if that was You, have Art come to me at the conclusion of this meeting and say, 'Shelly, there was a message for you in that teaching. Did you receive it?'"

At the conclusion of the meeting, Shelly felt an arm around his shoulder. He looked up and traced the arm to the body, it was attached to Art. Art asked, "Shelly, there was a message for you in that teaching. Did you receive it?"

Shelly was visibly undone. Art realized that he needed some time alone and told Shelly, that when he got his composure, to meet him outside where they could talk. Shelly remained standing in the tabernacle for a long while. He found it hard to believe that God had actually called him by name. And, that Art had voiced the same words that he had asked the Lord to have Art speak. He was stunned.

When he met Art outside, Shelly explained what had taken place. Art was amazed because he realized that God had spoken the same words to him. The Lord was calling Shelly to labor together with Art in Minnesota.

Art explained to Shelly that when the teacher had asked the question, to whom are you practically bound to in your home town, he heard the still small voice of the Lord say to him, "Shelly and his family belong here in Minnesota with you."

A struggle began in my heart when Shelly told me about his call. It felt like a tug of war. I had no desire to live on a farm in northern Minnesota, nor did I have a desire to live in a Christian community.

My heart ached thinking of the effect such a move would have on my parents, my brother, Robert, and his wife, Elaine, Rita and Norm, our Jewish friends and our family. Jesus brought division, but such a radical change of lifestyle would cause a chasm that could never be bridged.

Suzi was too young to realize what was happening. Scott and Dean cried when they learned we were moving to Minnesota, and I cried with them. What alternative did we have? The Lord was calling us and we had no choice but to obey.

That evening, at the conclusion of the meeting at Camp Dominion, I stood before the Lord and wept. "Lord, You know that I don't want to move here. I'm scared. How will we survive? How will my children adjust to such a radical lifestyle? What will happen to our relationship with my parents? What about my brother and his family? How will this move affect them? I need Your help, Lord!" I concluded my prayer by saying, "Even though I don't want to move here, Lord, if this is Your will for my life, I'm willing to obey."

Immediately, the war in my heart ceased. A deep peace filled my inner being, accompanied with assurance that the Lord would be with us and meet every one of our needs.

How can I thank you, Lord, for giving me peace when I had no peace? How can I thank you, Lord, for meeting me in my time of distress? You are the faithful One. You are worthy to be praised.

⊰૭⊱

When God calls, He is faithful to provide whatever it is you lack. He met me in my fears, He will meet you in yours. As He blessed me with peace, He will settle your soul also. Yield your will to the Lord and trust Him. You will be blessed, and He will make you...

A Blessing

No one can serve two masters.
Either he will hate the one
and love the other,
or he will be devoted to the one
and despise the other...
Matthew 6:24a

FOR SALE SIGN

Pray that your flight will not take place in winter
or on the Sabbath.
Matthew 24:20

It was during the winter of 1975-76 that Brother Michael came to visit us from Germany. He was one of the German brothers from the cell group of a monastic order which had purchased Arthur's home in New Jersey. Brother Michael was going through a deep struggle in his life, as he considered leaving the Brotherhood.

He wanted to visit Arthur in Minnesota to observe the community life on the farm. Michael did not want to travel alone and asked if Scott might accompany him, since it was during his winter school break. We thought it would be a meaningful experience for Scott to be with Brother Michael, so we agreed to let him go.

Their travels were filled with many adventures, and their time on the farm was meaningful for both of them. Scott experienced his heart being prepared for our eventual move. Seeing the lakes frozen over and the quietness of the farm during the cold winter month of February quieted his soul. He was at peace. For Brother Michael, it was a time of receiving a blessing from Arthur for his future.

We also had some days together with him before his return to Germany. He waited until the evening before his flight home to share his thoughts with us. Brother Michael appeared to be very nervous at the dinner table. He was having trouble communicating his thoughts because he felt that what he had to say would be difficult for us to receive. He believed that it was time for our move to Minnesota because the community had need of us.

My heart sank within me, as I recalled the Lord had me pray that our journey would not be in the winter. It was the middle of February. Shelly thanked Brother Michael for his honesty and prayed for the Lord to assist us in every detail.

Upon our return from the airport, Shelly bought a For Sale Sign and hammered it into the cold hard winter ground on our front lawn. It struck me funny seeing the For Sale Sign, since we lived on top of a hill, in a cul-de-sac, with only four other houses on our road. No one would see the sign unless they made a wrong turn or were visiting someone in one of the other four homes.

Our family gathered around our dining room table as Shelly prayed. He gave our house to the Lord, trusting He would send the one He desired to buy our home. He prayed that the sale price would not stand in the way. Shelly really believed the house would be sold in God's perfect time.

That very night, there was an electrical storm with thunder, lightning and hail. The following morning, we discovered the For Sale Sign had blown away, never to be found again. The roads were covered over with ice, so all schools were closed. Shelly's business trip to Boston was delayed as a result of the storm. All flights had been canceled.

Our phone rang very early that morning. It was a woman who had heard that we were selling our house. I was surprised and asked how she knew that our house was on the market. She said that word does get around. She asked if she and her husband could come that day to see our home. We set the time for their visit at noon.

At noon, the doorbell and telephone rang simultaneously. Shelly walked to the kitchen to answer the phone, as I walked to the front door. The woman was at the door with her husband and he looked very familiar to me. I asked if we had ever met. His response seemed odd to me. He said that I should know him. I asked where he was employed, thinking he might work in a store I frequented. His reply really shocked me. He said that he did not work at a store. He informed me that he was the new rabbi of our synagogue.

As we passed by the kitchen, Shelly looked the way I felt, shocked. I could not say which was open wider, his mouth or his eyes.

While I walked down the hall behind the rabbi and his wife, I looked up toward heaven smiling and thinking, "Lord, You sent the rabbi to buy our house. I can hardly contain myself. You really do have a wonderful sense of humor."

After viewing the main level, we walked down the stairs to the basement. It was then that the rabbi asked me how much we wanted for our home. When I told him the price, he replied that they could never afford to buy our house.

I realized the rabbi knew of our faith in Jesus, because we were the talk of the town. I felt to be open and direct with him. I told him that just last night, we had prayed and asked the Lord to send the one He desired to buy our home. Shelly prayed that the sale price would not stand in the way. I assured the rabbi that Shelly would agree, that if he and his dear wife desired to buy our home, they could have it for whatever price they could afford.

His wife looked as though she was about to faint. She kept pulling on the hem of his jacket, her expression spoke loud and clear —LET'S GET OUT OF HERE!

That very moment, Shelly came trotting down the stairs speaking these profound words, "What can I say but woe is me, I am undone!" Shelly repeated to the rabbi verbatim what I had said. The rabbi and his wife were visibly shaken, but asked if he could view the den one more time.

Scott was watching a Christian television program and as the rabbi put his foot on the threshold of the den, a song began:

"Save his soul, O Lord—Save his soul, O Lord—Save his soul..."

I held my breath trying so hard not to laugh. This event really resembled a scene from a Broadway comedy. The rabbi was in the den only for a very short while. He then scurried out of the house, taking his wife by her arm. He thanked us for our consideration as he shut the door quickly behind them.

I laughed and danced in our living room for almost half an hour. Shelly along with Scott, Dean and Suzi sat on the living-room floor, leaning against the wall watching me, speechless. I laughed and sang in the same melody as "Save His Soul, O Lord."

"You sent the rabbi to our house, O Lord"

I asked the Lord to remind me of this event if I should ever get depressed, so I might laugh and rejoice, remembering the day He sent the rabbi and his wife to buy our home.

After I settled down a bit, Scott told us that when the rabbi entered the den, he didn't look around the room, but hurried to the bookshelves and thumbed quickly through the titles. We never did hear from the rabbi again.

We decided not to get a broker to sell our home or put an ad in the newspaper. We were too frightened to do anything after the For Sale Sign had blown away. And, to be completely honest, I was not in any hurry to move to Minnesota. The timing of the Lord would be perfect. The house would sell in His time, not ours.

A physician phoned several months later, asking if he and his wife could come by to see our house. He told us that the rabbi had informed him it was on the market. When I saw how his wife loved our home, I really believed they would be the buyers. But, it did not happen for several months.

We did not hear from them again until the month of June. The doctor apologized for not getting back to us, because his wife had been ill. He asked if they could come that evening to talk with us and when they arrived, we went into the den. The doctor shared that the rabbi had revealed to him the amount we would have accepted for our home. Shelly and I looked at each other and smiled, not knowing how to respond.

Shelly explained that we had prayed for the Lord to send the one He had desired to purchase our home. Since the rabbi came the following morning, we agreed to give him the house at whatever price he could afford. That price would have been well below the market value. He explained that offer was for the rabbi only. Shelly told the doctor what we were asking for our home. He thanked us and he and his wife departed.

Shelly turned to me and said that he knew the doctor would phone us shortly to offer us a price for the house, right in the middle of what the rabbi could afford and what we were asking. He reminded me of his prayer, that price would not stand in the way. He believed that we should accept their offer when they called.

Shelly had barely finished speaking before the phone rang. As he walked slowly into the kitchen, he asked if I could agree and accept their offer. My eyes filled with tears as I said that I could agree with him. When Shelly answered the phone, I heard him say, "That will be fine. We will accept your offer."

The doctor did offer the amount right in the middle, just as Shelly had said he would. We completed the closing of the house by the end of June. We did not have a broker nor did we place an ad in the newspaper. We just had a For Sale Sign that blew away. Never to be found again!

∽⌒⌒

When God has a plan for your life, and reveals it to you, it will come to pass. Be encouraged, your answer to prayer will come…

Not Too Early—Not Too Late—Right On Time

Commit to the LORD whatever you do,
and your plans will succeed.
Proverbs 16:3

Part 2

The road to the farm

Our trailer with the addition

BEAMED CEILINGS

Look at the birds of the air;
they do not sow or reap or store away in barns,
and yet your heavenly Father feeds them.
Are you not much more valuable than they?
Matthew 6:26

One morning, while sitting on my couch in our den, I cried to the Lord letting Him know that I was frightened of the unknown. I asked Him to please answer me as I prayed:

"How are we going to survive in Minnesota? How are we going to feed our children? How are we going to clothe our children? How can I mail a letter? Where will I get the money for a stamp? Will I find money hanging on a tree? Should I go down to the lake, catch a fish and open its mouth for money? Let's get serious, Lord." Then, looking up at our large beautiful beamed ceilings, I asked, *"And Lord, will I ever see beamed ceilings again before I get to heaven?"*

The vision for the community in Minnesota was for everyone to live as the first century church.

All the believers were together
and had everything in common.
Selling their possessions and goods,
they gave to anyone as he had need.
Every day they continued to meet together in the temple courts.
They broke bread in their homes and ate together
with glad and sincere hearts.
Acts 2:44 - 46

79

Our home had been sold. Our debts paid and most of our possessions given away. We moved to the farm in Minnesota in July, 1976. A three-bedroom trailer, which Art described as rustic, was to be our new home. As we approached the farm, I remember feeling as if a rope was being pulled tightly around my neck. I felt as though I was going to my death and I remember thinking that if I ever wrote a book, I would not leave out this chapter.

> *... but the righteous will live by his faith—*
> *Habakkuk 2:4b*

> *Whoever finds his life will lose it,*
> *and whoever loses his life*
> *for my sake will find it.*
> Matthew 10:39

Riding down the long narrow driveway to the farm seemed like an eternity. Everyone at the community welcomed us warmly. Art asked if we would like to see our trailer. "By the way," he said, "I did not have the opportunity to tell you that we have not yet leveled your trailer. Also, we are in the process of digging a well for the trailers, so you will not have running water or electricity for awhile." Many different thoughts were racing so quickly through my head that my stomach was getting upset.

In front of the door to our trailer in the place of a porch were two old chairs stacked one on top of the other. Shelly was so kind as to allow me to be the first one to enter our new home. He lifted me up to the top of the chairs and I opened the torn screen door and looked around.

All the screens on the windows were torn. Cobwebs were on the walls and windows, and as I was about to pass out from the shock of it all, I looked up. Would you believe that The Ceilings Were Beamed!!! The still small voice of the Lord spoke clearly to my heart saying, "Now, June, if I can bring you Beamed Ceilings in a place like this, can I not feed your children? Can I not clothe your children? Can I not take care of all your needs?"

∽જી∾

The Lord has shown Himself faithful throughout the years to His promise. There has never been a time when we experienced a lack of food on our table or clothes on our backs. The provision of God for our family was always more than adequate. Trust the Lord without fear; He is trustworthy.

He Is Faithful To His Promise

Therefore I tell you,
do not worry about your life,
what you will eat or drink;
or about your body,
what you will wear.
Is not life more important than food,
and the body more important than clothes?
Matthew 6:25

KILLING YOUR IDOLS

For the word of God is living and active.
Sharper than any double-edged sword,
it penetrates even to dividing soul and spirit, joints and marrow;
it judges the thoughts and attitudes of the heart.
Hebrews 4:12

Before leaving Connecticut, Shelly and I had decided to put the belongings we were taking into storage, until we settled into the trailer. There was a battle going on in my heart over my fifty or so healthy, beautiful plants. My heart's desire was not to part with them. I realized that if I asked Shelly to rent a U-Haul to take the plants to Minnesota, he would absolutely refuse. I also realized there were basic needs for everyday life, such as dishes, silverware, pots, pans, towels, sheets... We could not possibly fit everything we needed in the trunk of our car. Taking that thought into consideration, I asked Shelly if we could rent a U-Haul and he agreed.

Deep within my heart of hearts however, I was primarily concerned about my plants as well as my pictures. I struggled with putting the pictures into storage. Nonetheless, I never made mention of the plants or the pictures to Shelly. At that time, I was not aware of manipulation or deception being sin. I was not even aware that I was being manipulative or deceptive. My actions were simply a way of life.

On July 2, 1976, we drove out of our driveway pulling a U-Haul, into which I had lovingly packed all my pictures and plants. We were beginning our journey of living by faith. There were uncertainties accompanied by a degree of fear, but one thing we knew for sure: the hand of the Lord was upon our family.

Wherever we stopped for the evening, we lined up all fifty plants. I carefully misted their leaves and lovingly watered them. Shelly was not very pleased with this procedure, but he was very gracious about it. I was thrilled when the plants survived the move; not one was lost. If I remember correctly, they were the first of our belongings to be placed in the trailer.

About two months later, my mother phoned from Florida saying she missed us and asked if we could possibly come for a visit. In the month of November, we received a check for $500 which at that time was enough to cover our driving expenses to Florida. We left for Florida the day after Christmas. One of the single sisters offered to take care of the plants and watch over our trailer while we were away.

We had a delightful time with my parents. The children enjoyed going to the beach, swimming in the ocean and making castles in the sand. It really was a treat for them, considering that back in Minnesota it was well below zero.

Bonnie, the single sister who was caring for our trailer, appeared troubled when we returned. I asked her if anything was wrong when she began to cry, "I'm so sorry. I'm so sorry." I could not imagine what had upset her so terribly. She went on to explain that while we were away, she had gone to Minneapolis to visit her parents and when she had returned, she discovered the electricity in our trailer had been turned off. All the plants froze.

My heart started pounding. I was so upset that I went into our bathroom for some privacy. I was devastated! My stomach was in knots over the loss of my beautiful, healthy green plants.

It was then that the Lord spoke to my heart, "June, thank Me for killing your idols!" I was speechless. I pondered a long while on the words that the Lord had just spoken to me. "Thank Me for killing your idols."

That was a valuable lesson and it transformed my way of thinking. The Lord cared so much for me that He would not allow manipulation and deceit to prevail in my life. For that, I am eternally grateful.

I asked Shelly to please forgive me for not being completely honest with him about renting the U-Haul. I also asked the Lord to forgive me for not trusting Him with the plants and pictures, as well as every aspect of life. I gave my pictures to the Lord along with everything that was dear to my heart. I realized then, it was better to suffer loss and gain Christ.

In the Lord's faithfulness, He brought new plants into the trailer. However, they were no longer my plants, they were His. I do not remember where they came from, but our trailer had large, beautiful, healthy green plants all the years that we lived on the farm. To this very day, even as I write, every home we have lived in has been filled with beautiful green plants and flowers, a reflection of the Lord's creation.

≪∙⩕∙≫

Are you troubled about losing something or someone you adore? Do you manipulate to get your own way? Is there something or someone who is preventing you from entering into His rest? Are you willing to surrender your life to God? By faith, surrender everything to the Lord and you will be set free. Ask the Lord to teach you how to delight yourself in Him and Him alone. The Lord desires you. He loves you and longs to teach you His ways.

His Love Is Better Than Wine—Or Plants ☺

All a man's ways seem innocent to him,
but motives are weighed by the LORD.
Proverbs 16:2

BLAMING OTHERS

Above all else, guard your heart, for it is the wellspring of life.
Proverbs 4:23

By the time September rolled around, there still was no running water or electricity in our trailer. We used a portable oil burner to heat water and to light the living room and kitchen area of the trailer. We had no choice but to use the outhouse. I found myself looking back at our life in Connecticut and grumbling in my heart about the living conditions on the farm.

There was only one washing machine, and it was at Inger's house. She had three children and shared her washer with all the families as well as the single men and women in the community. I was frustrated about the laundry arrangement, and many other things seemed to trouble me, too. The children adjusted well to our new way of life. Shelly did not appear to be disturbed by any of the inconveniences, although he would open the front door of our trailer each morning, look up to heaven and shout, "Get me out of here!" That seemed to get him through his days as he whistled praise songs and kept a smile on his face.

The children started school at the end of August and it was so cold when I woke them up, that I would cry. First thing in the morning, we would get water from the camp kitchen and heat it with our portable burner. Some of the water was used to wash and the rest we kept in a large jar for drinking or brushing our teeth. The outhouse continued to be a challenge for us, since we shared it with three other families and the single brothers.

Unsettling thoughts would race through my mind each morning, and it was always a battle to stop them. The thoughts that managed to remain throughout the day were: "If only the men responsible for working on the well were more diligent. If they were really doing their job, we would have water and electricity by now. Why is it taking them so long to finish the well? Why can't they see how inconvenient it is for so many people to use the same outhouse? What's wrong with them? The weather is so cold in the morning, it is difficult for the children to get up and get ready for school. How thoughtless can they be?"

Before the well was completed, our furniture arrived. Our trailer was really inviting once the screens had been fixed and the pictures were hung. Everything we brought with us had a place in the trailer. The curtains that once hung in our den in Connecticut, now dressed our windows in the living room, kitchen and dinette area. Our plants were the finishing touch that brought life and warmth to the trailer that was now home.

One September morning, it was so cold when I awoke, I could not feel my nose. My first thought of the day was, "How can I ask the children to get up from underneath their warm blankets and get dressed? It's freezing! If only the men were doing their job, we would have had heat by now."

The attitude of my heart was not right, but by the mercy of God my next thought was, "Please, Lord, forgive me for my attitude and soften my heart. If it is Your will for us to continue to live in these conditions, please give me the grace to accept it. Forgive me for grumbling in my heart against the men. Bless them for their labor of love in serving us in this way."

That very day, the well was completed. We now had heat, water and electricity. It was as though the Lord was waiting for me to change. I thanked God every time I turned on the lights. I thanked Him each time the fresh well water flowed out from the faucets. I realized that in America in this day and age, it was unusual to be thankful for heat, water and electricity. We take utilities for granted.

God was in the process of teaching me to have a grateful heart, and I was not even conscious of it.

My gratefulness for running water, however, began slowly dwindling. Using our faucet in the kitchen revealed that there was another problem; the faucet leaked. Again I thought, "Why is it not being fixed?" The dripping water was driving me crazy. I would complain to Shelly at least once a day. You can be sure of it. Frustration was becoming a way of life with me. Why was I not able to be patient? Why had I not learned my lesson? What was wrong with me?

At the same time, I was puzzled over a question asked by everyone who entered our trailer. We had a large painting of a woman wearing a straw hat with flowers that hung opposite the entrance door. Everyone who entered our trailer would ask if the picture was a painting of me. It was odd, because that same picture had hung in our hall in Connecticut for four years, yet no one had ever asked me that question. It happened so often that I became concerned over it.

One day, the Lord asked, "Do you want to be the first person people notice when they enter your trailer?" I replied, "No, Lord, my desire is for You to be the first one seen and for Your presence to be felt by each and every one who enters." I connected His question with the picture of the woman and concluded that it needed to be removed.

I asked Betty, who was Inger's helper and an artist, if she would be willing to paint "The Lord's Prayer" in calligraphy. I was planning to put "The Lord's Prayer" in the frame in place of the picture of the woman. Betty was so sweet and replied that she would love to do that for me in watercolors. I decided to leave the picture hanging on the wall until Betty completed the calligraphy.

The continual dripping of the faucet was becoming a greater challenge for me to overcome. It resulted in discord between Shelly and me. By this time, not only was I complaining, I was blaming Shelly for the faucet not being fixed. And, would you believe that I was scheduled to be the guest speaker at a meeting for women? How could I speak to women about Jesus in my condition?

I had been grumbling and complaining for weeks about that faucet and had barely gotten over being disgruntled about the well. And now this thing with the picture; I was feeling as though I should be removed, not the picture.

I decided to throw in the towel. I phoned Shelly at his office and asked him to forgive me for complaining about the faucet. He not only forgave me, he prayed for me and encouraged me to go to the women's meeting and be blessed in sharing the victory that God gives to us in every situation we face in life. My message to the women that morning was my very life.

... And the contentions of a wife are a constant dripping.
Proverbs 19:13b

The only word left out in that Scripture to describe my very life was faucet. All the women identified. No more nagging! We all prayed for the Lord to change us and give us the victory in Him.

When I returned home that day, would you believe, hanging on the wall in place of the picture of the woman with the straw hat was "The Lord's Prayer" in water-colors, adorned with the most beautiful tiny flowers. And the faucet no longer dripped.

∽⌇≻

"As you wait upon the LORD, you learn to see things from His perspective, move at His pace, and function under His directives. Waiting times are growing times and learning times. As you quiet your heart, you enter His peace; as you sense your weakness, you receive His strength; as you lay down your will, you hear His calling. When you mount up, you are being lifted by the wind of His Spirit... When you move ahead, you are sensitive to His timing. When you act, you give yourself only to the thing He has asked you to do."
By Roy Hession

Be Still And Know That He Is God

Wait for the LORD;
be strong and take heart
and wait for the LORD.
Psalm 27:14

REMOVING OBSTACLES

You want something but don't get it.
You kill and covet, but you cannot have what you want.
You quarrel and fight.
You do not have, because you do not ask God.
James 4:2

Two young women came to live with us about a year after we moved to the farm. Kathy was a young woman from the Twin Cities and Cathy was my friend from Connecticut who baked and served the cake for the First Seder. Shelly and I slept in the living room on a couch that opened up to a king-size bed. Scott and Dean slept in our bedroom, and we gave the two girls their bedroom. Suzi was comfortable in her own little room.

All the trailers had an entrance room added for their winter gear. I desired to have an open porch by our entrance door, so our addition was to be built by another door near the boys' bedroom.

The men were beginning the construction of the addition on the day that I was scheduled to do the shopping in town. When I returned, I discovered the addition was being built with a large tree as part of the far wall. If there was a bad storm and the tree uprooted, the boys' beds would be the direct target under the fall.

I asked the men to please remove the tree or not build an addition to our trailer. They all seemed to ignore my appeal as they continued building the addition. What added to my frustration was that Shelly was one of those men! He was not at all concerned about the tree.

I went to my bedroom and closed the door behind me. I got down on my knees by our bed and asked the Lord to please calm my heart. My first thought was my attitude. It was definitely not a grateful one nor respectful to the men, and I felt ashamed of myself. The men really were trying to help us. I walked out and asked them to please forgive me for my attitude, and they were gracious to me. They nodded their heads in agreement.

I returned to our bedroom, kneeled again by my bed and prayed, "Please, Lord, protect the boys from any impending danger and give me a peace about leaving the tree as part of the wall. If it is Your will for the tree to be removed, please, Lord, change the hearts of the men."

Before I finished my prayer, Shelly opened our bedroom door and asked, "Have you been praying? The men have decided to remove the tree, and they are extending the addition another four feet."

༺ঔ৵

Take courage if there is an obstacle in your life. If it is a physical obstacle, as my tree, or a spiritual mountain—call upon the Lord. He will hear your cry. He will remove the obstacle or give you the grace to bear it.

The Lord Is The Master Remover Of Obstacles

But he gives us more grace.
That is why Scripture says:
"God opposes the proud
but gives grace to the humble."
James 4:6

LIVING BY FAITH

I was young and now I am old,
yet I have never seen the righteous forsaken
or their children begging bread.
Psalm 37:25

The construction for the addition to our trailer was progressing. We needed funds to purchase materials like: windows, paneling, flooring, paint, etc.... We needed a bed or sleeper couch for the two girls who were living with us. Suzi needed curtains for her room and a cover for her bed. On my personal list of needs was a washing machine. I recognized these needs as another opportunity to experience the provision of the Lord.

Kathy, one of the girls living with us, asked if she could pray with me for money for our needs. She was very specific in her prayer and mentioned all the above items.

The following day, there was a knock at our door. It was a jeweler from the Twin Cities with his wife and children. The men working on the addition waved to our guests as they walked into the trailer. It was noon, so I invited them to join us for lunch.

This was the first time the family had visited the farm and they desired to take a tour of the property. After lunch, I phoned Mark and asked if he would be willing to accompany them as they toured the grounds.

The jeweler thanked me for lunch and asked, "Before we leave we would like to give a donation for this work. To whom should I write the check?" I told him to make out the check to Ben Israel Ministries. He put the folded check in my hand and I thanked him.

I hugged the jeweler, his wife and children and we said our good-byes. I put the folded check on our living room table.

About an hour had passed when the jeweler knocked at our door again. He told me that he and his wife had prayed, and they wanted to give the check to our family for our needs. I thanked him for being so kind, but told him that the Lord took care of our needs. He replied, "Then use the check for anything you desire; the money is for you." I thanked him for being so kind, yet deep within my heart I never considered using his check for our family. As he drove away, I walked to the table and unfolded the check. I could not believe my eyes. I was stunned. The check was for $1,500. In 1977, that amount was sufficient to cover all of our needs.

Kathy was in Suzi's bedroom sewing. When I told her about the jeweler and what he had said about the check, her expression changed. She stopped sewing, looked up at me with her beautiful blue eyes and said, "June, do you remember what I prayed yesterday? That money is for you." My knees felt weak; I had forgotten about her prayer.

Shelly phoned home that evening from out of state. He was accompanying Art on a ministry trip. I told him about the jeweler giving me a check made out to Ben Israel and wanting it to be for our family, to use for our personal needs. I also told him about Kathy's prayer. His immediate response was that we could not use a penny of that money because the check had been made out to Ben Israel Ministries. I must confess, I was a little disappointed. However, I understood why he felt that way.

As I hung up the phone, the still small voice of the Lord said to me that if Shelly did not allow me to use the $1,500, He would give me $3,000. When I told Kathy and Cathy about our phone conversation and what the Lord had said to me, Cathy's face turned pale. I asked her what was wrong. She told me that her tax refund was $3,000. I laughed and assured her that the $3,000 from her tax return was her money, and she need not worry. The Lord would provide the $3,000 for us if we could not use the check.

Shelly phoned the following day. He had told Arthur about the jeweler and his desire for the use of the funds to be for our family. Arthur told him that the check was for us and we were to do with it as we saw fit.

And so we did. We purchased the material for Suzi's room and Kathy designed and made a beautiful comforter, with pillowcase and curtains to match. We bought everything needed for the addition: a washing machine, a sleeper couch, carpeting, paneling and a large picture window that allowed us to view the beauty of the Minnesota woodlands. It was the only window in our trailer that was not covered with plastic during the cold winter months. And there was money to spare, so we bought winter boots for some of the children in the community.

It took time for me to learn to completely put my trust in the Lord. Many years later, Suzi used the comforter and curtains to decorate her daughter Sarah's nursery. The sleeper couch is in my office and looks as good as the day we purchased it. God is our provider in ways past finding out. These items are a reminder to me of how the Lord kept my people's clothing from wearing out when He brought them out of the land of Egypt.

∼⊹∼

If the Lord is calling for you to trust Him in a deeper way, I promise you that He will not disappoint you.

His Provision Will Come—At The Perfect Time Wait And See

And my God will meet all your needs
according to His glorious riches
in Christ Jesus.
Philippians 4:19

With Joy Serve You Only

Fill my heart with joy
Let me see You in all I do
To reach out and serve others
As You served O Servant King
Help me Lord to see You only

When my hands are weak
When my heart is unfaithful
Change me Lord to be one with You
To repent and trust You with all
Help me Lord to see You only

Eternal One help me to look up
That joy might come and fill my heart
That joy might come and restore my soul
Make me whole in You
Help me Lord to see You only

Joy comes in the morning
The Joy of the Lord is my strength
Let me shout for Joy in Your victory
Open my eyes dear Lord to see
And with Joy serve You only

June Volk

A SERVANT'S HEART

...Worship the Lord your God, and serve him only.
Matthew 4:10b

About a month after we arrived at Ben Israel, it was decided that Arthur and his family needed a season of rest away from the community. They were offered a home in Kansas City for a year. We all knew that it was the will of the Lord and each one of us had peace in our heart with their move. However, their absence would be a challenge for all of us. Inger served the community in practical ways and I learned this very important lesson as a result of her absence.

The community ate a Shabbat meal together every Friday evening. The ladies were asked to help prepare the food for the Shabbat dinners at the camp kitchen. We were scheduled to meet there early each Friday morning.

The first Friday morning after Inger had moved, I walked down to the camp kitchen with Debbie, who was single, to help prepare the Shabbat meal. Upon our arrival, one of the single brothers, Jeff, asked if we were ready for the chickens.

Within a few minutes, I heard the loudest shrieking and cackling sounds. All I could think was, "Oh, no! I'm a city girl. Could it be? I always bought my chicken at the supermarket, how could this be happening to me?" It was happening alright.

I asked Jeff to please be so kind as to pluck the feathers and cut the chickens for me. He chuckled when he said he would gladly do it. It was my first experience of flavoring warm chickens before putting them in the oven. I must confess though, they were the most delicious chickens I had ever tasted.

The following Friday morning, Debbie and I walked down to the kitchen, and I was hoping to see some of the ladies waiting to cook the meal with us. Not one lady was there. After putting on my apron, I became agitated as we started to prepare the meal. I said to Debbie, "This is not right. All the women ate the meal last week, yet they did not help prepare it nor did they help with the clean-up. And, here we are again, preparing the meal alone." I untied my apron and put it on the counter and said, "If they don't help cook, there will be no meal."

Debbie, gifted with wisdom, responded, "June, who are you cooking for? If you are cooking for people, you will always have a problem. If you are cooking for the Lord, He will always bless you and send you all the help you need. June, let your heart be at peace. Serve the Lord with all your heart, not men. Serve Him only." Those words have been hidden deep within my heart all these years. Thank you, Debbie, for your wise counsel.

I put on my apron again and continued preparing the meal with Debbie. When we finished, I heard the still small voice say, "Go home, shower, wash your hair and wear your finest dress and remember, as you serve each person tonight, you will be serving Me."

> *The King will reply,*
> *"I tell you the truth,*
> *whatever you did for one of the least*
> *of these brothers of mine,*
> *you did for me."*
> Matthew 25:40

The Lord gave me an assignment that day to provoke my sisters to jealousy by serving Him with joy.

The following year, I not only cooked and served the Shabbat meals alone, but I did the same for Sunday lunches that followed our service. When Inger returned to the community, we alternated cooking for Friday dinners and Sunday lunches. I felt privileged to serve with Inger. The Lord had changed my heart to see the joy in serving Him.

I was also responsible for hospitality. We had people visit the community from all over the world. My responsibility was to clean and prepare the guest trailers and the House of Judah, down the road at Camp Dominion, with clean sheets and towels. Out of the kindness of their hearts Debbie and Vera who were single sisters assisted me.

Many years later, I discovered some of the women resented me because they thought I wanted to be in control. It hurt my heart that I had given them that impression. I cried and asked the Lord to help me to change my ways. I had failed Him as His servant. So I thought.

One morning, Inger phoned and said, "Junsey, I believe it is time for the ladies at Ben Israel to grow up. I think they should begin by taking responsibility for hospitality and also, preparing the Friday *Shabbat* dinners and Sunday lunches. How do you feel about that?" I laughed as I told her that I thought that was a wonderful idea.

I then heard the still small voice of the Lord speak to me, "Remember when I asked you to provoke your sisters to jealousy by serving Me with joy? Let your heart be at peace."

His master replied,
"Well done, good and faithful servant!
You have been faithful with a few things;
I will put you in charge of many things.
Come and share your master's happiness!"
Matthew 25:21

❧❧

Serve the Lord with gladness and thanksgiving. If you should find yourself suffering for doing good, *rejoice and be glad for great is your reward in heaven.* And please, whatever you do, do not give up loving Him, serving Him and seeing His goodness—no matter what may come your way.

God Sees—God Hears—God Cares

Blessed are you when men cast insults at you,
and persecute you,
and say all kinds of evil against you falsely,
on account of Me.
Matthew 5:11

For it is commendable if a man bears up under the pain
of unjust suffering because he is conscious of God.
I Peter 2:19

THE BULLY

Before a word is on my tongue you know it completely, O LORD.
Psalm 139:4

Our children attended school in Cass Lake, a small town located on the Chippewa Indian Reservation. Scott was going into the seventh grade. The junior high and high school students were in the same building. It was a tough town and a tough high school that suffered from gang wars and rapes as common-place events. At that time, the principal carried a gun to school.

Scott was a high achiever, but was placed in a slow learning class because we had arrived after the official registration date. After the first day of school, Scott appeared troubled. His classmates had harassed him throughout the entire day. Scott was sensitive and was suffering deeply and my heart ached for him. The problem intensified because of his good grades provoking his classmates to tease him constantly. The tension grew between his classmates and especially with one boy who bullied him relentlessly. On one occasion, the bully pushed Scott down a flight of stairs.

One morning, during our prayer meeting, the principal phoned and suggested that we bring Scott home for the day. I cried out, "Lord, You called us to live here. You had us register the children in public school. You know all things and I know that You work all things to the good. Why are You allowing this to happen? Please, Lord, help Scott through this trial."

I felt sick to my stomach as Scottie sat on his bed, crying. I spoke gently to him, "My heart hurts for you, Scottie, for having so much trouble at school with your classmates. I know that Jesus is Lord of your life and He knows everything about you. If He is permitting this persecution, there must be a reason. Can we pray and ask the Lord why He has allowed you to suffer in this manner?"

Scottie's response surprised me, "Mom, I have prayed. The Lord has revealed to me why He allowed this to happen. Last year, I teased the kindergarten students as they got off the school bus and acted like the bully. Jesus wanted me to experience the hurt I caused by my actions, so that I would never treat anyone that way again."

It amazed me that Scottie had asked the Lord why he was being persecuted and I was comforted to hear that Jesus had already answered him. Scottie continued, "I asked the Lord to forgive me and heal the hearts of the children I teased. I am really sorry, Mom." I cried with Scottie and we prayed together and I assured him of God's promise:

If we confess our sins,
he is faithful and just
and will forgive us our sins
and purify us from all unrighteousness.
I John 1:9

We asked the Lord to be merciful and deliver Scottie from the bully. Could it be that Scottie could be transferred to another class? We knew that it was against school policy to transfer a student after the session began; however, would God make a way?

The principal phoned the next morning informing us that he had a major problem and asked if we could help resolve it. The state board was investigating discrimination at Cass Lake High School. One seventh grade class had only girls. He decided to take two boys from each of the other seventh grade classes and put them with the girls. He asked permission to transfer Scottie into that class, and we were elated at the solution for Scott's problem. So we thought!

When Scottie came home from school, he was laughing as he said, "Mom, you are not going to believe this. Who do you think was transferred out of my class with me? Would you believe the bully?

Mom, he talked to me all day. He didn't have a friend in that class and now we are friends."

Scott remained friends with the bully throughout his years at Cass Lake High School. In his senior year, Shelly coached the baseball team and the bully played side by side with Scott. Shelly prayed with the team before each game and at the end of the season, he gave a Bible to each of the players. The bully witnessed the love and forgiveness of God through their relationship.

Scottie has never forgotten his encounter with the bully. He learned valuable lessons at a very young age. He learned that if we ask the Lord, He will reveal our hidden sins. He learned to repent and be sorry for his sin, and he learned that the Lord desired to deliver him and to set him free. He learned to forgive as he was forgiven and also learned to love others as God loves us. To this day, Scottie is a gentle soul and very sensitive to how he treats others, both in word and in deed.

≪⌾≫

Do you have hidden sins? Is there a difficult person in your life? Have you asked the Lord why He has allowed that person to be in your life? Be encouraged, the Lord will answer you and He will teach you, as He taught Scott, many new lessons.

Be Mindful Of How You Treat Others

You have heard that it was said,
"Love your neighbor and hate your enemy."
But I tell you:
"Love your enemies and pray for those who persecute you,
that you may be sons of your Father in heaven ..."
Matthew 5:43 - 45a

105

Search me, O God, and know my heart;
test me and know my anxious thoughts.
See if there is any offensive way in me,
and lead me in the way everlasting.
Psalms 139: 23, 24

IS CASS LAKE ENOUGH

Whether it is favorable or unfavorable,
we will obey the LORD our God,...
Jeremiah 42:6a

There was great anticipation at the farm. News had come that the headquarters of Ben Israel Ministries might be moved to Holland and the thought of living in Europe was very exciting for our entire family.

A meeting was scheduled to discuss this prospect for the community. To my surprise, it was decided that if the base for the work was to be moved to Holland, our family would remain on the farm. I was devastated.

We were born and raised in New York City. What did we know about farming? Besides, along with our burden for the kingdom of God, we had a burden for our Jewish people. There was not a Jew among the one thousand and one persons living in all of Cass Lake. Talk about being frustrated! You may be sure that I cried and prayed about this predicament. During a time of deep prayer, the Lord asked me, "Is Cass Lake Enough for you?" In tears I replied, "No, Lord. Cass Lake is not enough."

Several days later, I had an early morning appointment and I had asked Scottie to please make his bed and straighten up his room. I was gone for several hours and when I returned, I was surprised that his bedroom was still messy. I asked him why he had not made his bed or cleaned up his room.

He answered, "But Mom, I vacuumed the living room and polished the furniture. I vacuumed your bedroom and did the wash. I even cleaned the bathroom. Why are you so upset with me?"

I calmed down and thanked Scottie for trying to help me. I realized that he meant well and I did appreciate all he had accomplished. I told him that the next time I asked him to clean up his room, it would be best for him to do that first. Then, if he wanted to help me further and clean the remainder of the trailer, that would be a blessing for me.

I then heard the still small voice of the Lord say to me, "Is Cass Lake Enough for you? Why are you not willing to do what I have set before you? Then, if you wanted to help Me further, that would be a blessing for Me."

The community never did move to Holland, but I learned a very important lesson. It is a blessing to serve the Lord and relieve Him of one of His concerns by doing what He asks.

✂✁

What is the "Cass Lake" in your life? Lord, please teach us to be faithful and to serve You each day with everything You put before us with all of our hearts. Help us to obey You in the little things that we might be faithful in much.

The Lord Has Need Of Thee

Whoever can be trusted with very little
can also be trusted with much, ...
Luke 16:10a

PRESS DOWN DEEPER

Blessed is the man who trusts in the LORD
And whose trust is the LORD.
Jeremiah 17:7

Two or three years had passed and I found myself experiencing spiritual dryness. It was as though I was walking through a tunnel, knowing there was light at the beginning and light at the end. However, I found myself in the middle of the tunnel where there was total darkness. My communion with the Lord was drying up and I did not understand why.

I asked the Lord to search my heart for hidden sin. I asked the Lord if there was a broken relationship that I needed to mend; I sought His face day and night. I found myself in distress because the Lord was silent. I honestly do not recall how long I remained in that condition, but I do remember the fog in which I found myself.

One fall morning, there was a knock at my door; it was my friend, Gail. The Lord in His faithfulness had sent me His messenger, a gifted teacher of the Word. She lived in Grand Rapids, which was well over an hour's drive away.

It was a beautiful brisk day and Gail asked if we could take a walk together. The sun was shining so brightly that it lit up all the trees in the northern woods. The leaves on the trees were at the height of their autumn colors. We walked in silent meditation for quite awhile, down the narrow dirt road that I had walked so many times before.

Gail mused at some of the trees standing erect while others were tilted and asked me what my thoughts were as to why that was so.

Although I had walked that road so many times, I never did take note of how many of those trees were tilted.

As I pondered Gail's question, she went on to explain to me that in the state of Minnesota there are 10,000 lakes with an abundance of trees. Because of the endless supply of water, the roots do not go down deep into the soil. Therefore, when the winds and storms come, they cause the trees to tilt. On the other hand, in the state of Nebraska, there are few lakes and very few trees. The trunks of the trees are huge and the trees stand erect, because the roots press down deeper into the soil to find their source of water.

Gail told me that the Lord desired for me to press down deeper into Him. There are seasons when the Lord appears to be silent, not necessarily as a result of your sin. She tried to encourage me to persevere, so that my roots might go deeper in the Messiah.

⋘⋙

Are you going through a dry spell? Do you trust the Lord for light at the end of your tunnel? If sin is the cause of your dryness, repent, so that times of refreshing might come. Be encouraged. If the Lord is silent and your conscience is clear, this is your season to press down deeper so that His Life might spring up.

Seek The Lord
The Fountainhead Of Your Supply

He will be like a tree planted by the water
that sends out its roots by the stream.
It does not fear when heat comes;
its leaves are always green.
It has no worries in the year of drought
and never fails to bear fruit.
Jeremiah 17:8

THE SWINE FLU

And he said:
"I tell you the truth, unless you change
and become like little children,
you will never enter the kingdom of heaven."
Matthew 18:3

During the winter of 1976, there was a terrible epidemic of the swine flu. Every few minutes on television or radio, warnings about signs and symptoms were given. Should paralysis occur, it could be fatal.

Shelly was on a ministry trip with the elders of the community and Suzi was very sick with a high fever. I was extremely concerned about her condition.

On one of the news flashes, there was a warning that numbness was the initial symptom of paralysis. A few minutes after the news flash, Suzi cried out from her bedroom that it felt like her arms and legs were falling asleep. That was a graphic description for a six-year-old explaining numbness. I panicked!

I asked Scott and Dean to find one of the men to anoint Suzi with oil and pray before taking her to the hospital. Richard Cushing came to our trailer a short while later. He had not been to a doctor in years, because he believed he should trust in the Lord for sovereign healings. To be honest, anyone who did not go to doctors intimidated me and I would get very nervous.

I explained Suzi's physical condition to Richard and told him that I had planned to take her to the emergency room after he prayed for her. He was very sensitive to my feelings. He tried to encourage me by letting me know that he believed that mothers had a natural instinct and knew what was best for their child. He was willing to help me in any way that he could.

Suzi's fever was very high when Richard walked into her bedroom. He was very gentle with her and asked several questions before he anointed her with oil to pray. I will never forget their conversation. Richard asked Suzi if she believed that Jesus loved her. Suzi answered that she did believe that Jesus loved her. Richard asked her if she believed that Jesus could heal her. Suzi responded that she did believe Jesus could heal her.

Richard went on to explain that some of the closest apostles to Jesus suffered in their bodies and were not healed. Peter was an apostle and had the gift of healing. His gift was so powerful that even when people walked in his shadow, they were healed. Timothy was a disciple of the Lord and he had a stomach problem. The Scriptures never mentioned Timothy's stomach being healed and he knew Peter who had the gift of healing. Paul, another great leader, had a thorn in his flesh and he asked the Lord to remove it three times. The Scriptures say that the thorn was put there to keep him humble and it caused Paul to be more dependent upon Jesus.

Richard asked Suzi that if Jesus did not heal her, would she still love Him. She responded quickly that she would still love Jesus even if He did not heal her. Richard asked her if Jesus did not heal her, would she know that He still loved her very much. Very softly, Suzi answered that she would know Jesus still loved her. Richard told Suzi that he was ready to pray.

He anointed her forehead with olive oil and prayed for the Lord to touch her body and heal her. He asked for mercy and then prophesied, "I see Suzi's angel pleading for her life before the throne of God."

While Richard prayed, my anxiety lifted and a deep peace filled my heart. It was then that I knew I should not take Suzi to the hospital. Doctors were watching their patients die because there was not a cure for the swine flu. I believed that Suzi was in the hands of the Great Physician. I thanked Richard and told him that I no longer felt the need to take Suzi to the emergency room.

Scott and Dean called me into their bedroom where I found them crying. They pleaded with me, telling me that they didn't want Suzi to die. I told them that I didn't want her to die either. As we cried together, we prayed and pleaded with the Lord to please be merciful and to show Himself faithful to us once again.

Several hours had passed when Suzi came out of her bedroom, walking very slowly and speaking very softly. She told me that her legs and arms did not feel like they were falling asleep any more. I picked Suzi up and held her in my arms, very close to my heart for a long while before carrying her back to bed. Her fever had gone down considerably.

Suzi's healing was not completed instantly, but her illness no longer seemed life-threatening. I believe the Lord touched Suzi and healed her when Richard prayed, even though it was several weeks before the infection completely left her body.

Suzi's child-like faith touched my heart. The questions that Richard asked are questions we should ask ourselves. Suzi's affliction changed my life and the way I handle threatening situations. Thank you, Lord, that you can give peace when there is no peace. Thank you for Your Shalom that keeps us.

⊱⊰

Is your heart open for a change during life threatening situations? Are you willing to entrust your life or the life of your loved one to the Lord? The Lord will direct you to go to a doctor or a hospital or to pray and wait. Are you listening for His voice? He is the only One who can bring you peace when there is no peace. Listen for His voice and obey.

He Is Sar Shalom—The Prince of Peace

...and a little child will lead them.
Isaiah 11:6b

THE FLORIST SHOP

Then He touched their eyes, saying,
"Be it done to you according to your faith."
Matthew 9:29

What a treat it was having lunch in Bemidji with my dear sisters and friends, Kathy and Michelle, who were part of The Christian Family Community. Someone had sent me money, so I was going to pay for Kathy and Michelle's meal. During lunch, we discussed two other good friends of ours, Marti and Inger. We realized that they both needed some tender loving care.

I thought I heard the still small voice of the Lord tell me to go to the nearest florist shop and buy two bud vases with three red roses in each. I was to give one bud vase to Inger and the other to Marti with a note from the Lord. The note was to read: Jesus loves you very much and He sees your struggles.

That was a wonderful idea. However, after paying for lunch I would have no money. I asked the Lord how I could buy the flowers without money. He did not answer me. I told Kathy and Michelle what I believed the Lord had said and they, too, thought it was a great idea.

When I told them I did not have the money for the flowers, their facial expressions changed dramatically. Kathy asked me the same question I had asked the Lord, "How are you going to buy the flowers without money?" I told her that I didn't know, but the Lord would make the way to pay for them. Besides, we needed some adventure in our lives.

I must confess I was somewhat nervous when we entered the florist shop. The girl behind the counter seemed excited to see me and I could not understand why. I didn't even know her. Excitedly, she told me that I was the lady she always saw at Pamida, a miniature Wal-Mart. Funny, I didn't remember seeing her. She said that I made her feel good because I always smiled at her. She wanted to know why I was always so happy.

I turned quickly to glance at Kathy and Michelle to catch their expressions. With a smile on my face, I turned back to the girl behind the counter and told her it was because I loved Jesus. I asked her if she knew Jesus could bring joy into her life also. That seemed to end our conversation.

I then ordered the two bud vases. My friends appeared uneasy about what would happen when it came time for me to pay the bill. I must confess that my knees were shaking underneath my long skirt.

As Sue, my newfound friend behind the counter was making up the two bud vases, her mother walked over to talk with us. I was not aware at the time that Sue was the owner's daughter. Would you believe that her mother looked me straight in the eye when she told me that Mother's Day and the high school prom were on the same day that year, which was most unusual. She said that they were short-handed at the florist shop and asked me if I would like to work for that week. She said they could not pay me with cash, but she would exchange flowers for my labor. And, she would begin the exchange with the two bud vases.

Kathy and Michelle's eyes widened, as their mouths dropped open. They appeared flushed, as though they were about to faint. Lord, You are awesome! I told Sue's mother that I would love to help her in the florist shop the week of Mother's Day.

Inger and Marti received their bud vases and notes from the Lord and were blessed. Kathy, Michelle and I were excited to see the Lord intervene. I also had the privilege of working in the florist shop before each Mother's Day for many more years which enabled me to send my mother beautiful plants and flowers. Sue came to faith in Jesus and her best friend, who worked at the jail, also got saved.

From the florist shop to the jail, the gospel was traveling across town. And remember it all began with an empty pocket, the still small voice, and two bud vases with three roses in each.

⋐⋒⋑

Has the Lord ever called you to something that seemed impossible for you to accomplish? Don't be afraid to step out in faith and obey His voice. Trust Him with all your heart and remember, do not lean on your own understanding. Obey His still small voice and your eyes will be opened to see the Lord at work.

The Lord Will Make—A Way
Where There Seems To Be—No Way

And their sight was restored.
Jesus warned them sternly,
"See that no one knows about this."
But they went out and spread the news
about him all over that region.
Matthew 9:30, 31

IT'S ME, JUNEY

Whatever you do, work at it with all your heart,
as working for the Lord, not for men,
since you know that you will receive an inheritance
from the Lord as a reward.
It is the Lord Christ you are serving.
Colossians 3:23, 24

E ric Beebe, Art and Mary's youngest son, was my special friend. He would walk from the farm to our trailer to visit. Although I knew it was Eric when he knocked at the door, I would ask in a melodic tone, "Who is it?" He would reply in his inimitable way, "It's me, Juney!" Several years ago, I saw Eric with his wife and new baby boy. We had not seen each other in over sixteen years. He had grown into such a handsome young man, well over six-feet-tall. He hugged me tight as he leaned over and whispered in my ear, "It's me, Juney!" I had a lump in my throat. It touched my heart to think that after all these years, Eric still remembered our special times together.

WHEN ERIC was three years old, I baby-sat for him with his two friends, Sorney and Gracie. Their sister, Faith, was six years old and was suffering with a malignant brain tumor. Faith loved the Lord with all her heart, soul, mind and strength. Whenever Faith needed chemotherapy treatments, I would take care of Sorney and Gracie.

One morning during breakfast, I noticed that Eric was not eating. I had baked cookies for dessert and told Eric that if he did not finish his breakfast, he could not have a cookie. He assured me that it was fine with him; he was not hungry. Sorney and Gracie emptied their plate and I gave them each a cookie and they all went into the addition of the trailer to play.

A short time after I sent the children into the addition to play I decided to check my wash in the washing machine when I overheard Eric whispering: "Sorney, Sorney, go tell Juney you want another cookie. Don't tell her it's for me." Then I heard the still small voice say to me, "And, June, I hear every word you speak also."

❖❖

We are just like little children. May this vignette be a reminder to you, as it has been for me, to consider what we speak and realize the motive of our heart. Let us remember that *out of the abundance of the heart, the mouth speaks.*

> *May the words of my mouth*
> *and the meditation of my heart*
> *be pleasing in your sight,*
> *O LORD,*
> *my Rock and my Redeemer.*
> Psalm 19:14

SORNEY AND GRACIE were playing together with Eric. They were coloring in the addition to our trailer, while I was preparing lunch.

A short time passed when Gracie came running into the kitchen very excitedly, waving her drawing, saying, "Juney, Juney, I made this picture just for you because I love you." I picked up Gracie and twirled her around and around and said, "Oh, Gracie, I love you so much too. Thank you sweetheart and I love your picture. I am going to tape it on the refrigerator so everyone can see it."

About ten minutes passed when Eric came running into the kitchen, waving the picture he had just made saying, "Juney, Juney, I made this picture just for you because I love you. Can you put my picture on the refrigerator next to Gracie's?" I could not believe my ears, or my eyes. Eric Beebe was teaching me another lesson!

It was then I heard the still small voice of the Lord say, "Do you serve Me because you love Me or because you want everyone to see?"

ᥓᥓ

Lord, help us to remember this admonition and serve You because we love You, and not for the recognition of men.

> *May those who love your salvation*
> *always say,*
> *"Let God be exalted!"*
> Psalm 70:4

ERIC'S PARENTS were in Europe on a ministry trip and I was caring for him and two of his brothers. Kathy and Cathy were still living with us, so our trailer was overflowing with youngsters.

I had finished putting away the breakfast dishes and was taking the wash out of my dryer. I was exhausted, realizing it was not one of my better days, and it was not yet seven-thirty in the morning. I was grumbling in my heart, not exactly feeling grateful.

I still had to dress Eric for the prayer meeting, which would begin within fifteen minutes, and I was not even finished folding the wash, nor had I taken my shower. It looked like I would never be able to make the morning prayer meeting. So I thought!

Eric was playing with a car, brushing it back and forth in a rhythmic beat. He was saying something, but I had tuned him out. The Lord was trying to get my attention as I heard, "Listen! Listen!"

As I was grumbling in my heart, I tried to concentrate on what Eric was saying. It took some time until I could hear Eric's words clearly, "Just praise the Lord. Just praise the Lord. Just praise the Lord." The rhythmic beat had a message and Eric continued saying, "Just praise the Lord," until I received the message.

When I obeyed and began to praise the Lord, the grumbling in my heart instantly ceased. I asked the Lord to please forgive me for my grumbling and continued to sing praises to Him aloud. Peace returned to my heart and I was filled with thanksgiving. So once again I want to thank you, Lord, for meeting me in my need. You always do show Yourself faithful.

❧❧

Everything surely does change when you sing praises to the Lord. Try it and see what happens!

> *From the lips of children and infants*
> *you have ordained praise*
> *because of your enemies,*
> *to silence the foe*
> *and the avenger.*
> Psalm 8:2

ONCE AGAIN, I found myself a bit overwhelmed. A few days after the praise the Lord incident, everything I tried to accomplish was going wrong. It was really discouraging me. Suddenly, I had what I thought was a crazy idea, until I tried it and it worked.

I looked at Eric and asked him if he would like to help me sweep Satan out of the trailer. Eric laughed and replied in his usual fashion, "Sure, Juney." I got my broom and started sweeping. I opened every closet and swept, telling him to get out. I told Satan that we belong to Jesus and there is no place for him in our trailer. After sweeping every closet, I opened the door and swept Satan out of the trailer.

Eric and I laughed and danced together, singing praises to the Lord. Peace returned to the trailer and everything seemed to calm down. I was able to accomplish what needed to be done. Eric played and was very happy and content for the remainder of that day.

A short time later, Eric's mother was struggling through a difficult day. Eric asked if she knew what I did when everything went wrong. Mary replied, "No, Hon, what does Juney do?" He fetched their broom and said that I sweep Satan right out of my closets. Then I open my front door and sweep him out of my trailer. And, that is exactly what they did. After the sweep, Mary and Eric laughed together, sang praises to the Lord and danced with joy.

৯৯৯

This is a needed reminder: we do have an adversary. Are you having a difficult day? Are you feeling discouraged? Don't let the adversary keep you from praising the Lord. Get your broom and start to sweep. Sing to the Lord and praise Him with thanksgiving in your heart. Your day will take a turn, because you have changed in His Presence.

In His Presence Is Fullness Of Joy

You have made known to me the path of life;
you will fill me with joy in your presence,
with eternal pleasures at your right hand.
Psalm 16:11

MRS. LAMB

Come and see the works of God,
Who is awesome in His deeds toward the sons of men.
Psalm 66:5

This Is Dedicated To The Memory Of Mrs. Lamb

Through the years, Shelly and I have met some of the Lord's choicest saints and Mrs. Lamb was one such person. Each summer our family would drive back East where we were reunited with old friends and family. It was on one of these trips that we met Mrs. Lamb.

Shelly preached at Pastor Andrew's church and after the service, Mrs. Lamb invited us to her home for lunch. She appeared to be a gentle soul in her mid-seventies.

During our time together, we asked Mrs. Lamb about her late husband. Her eyes lit up and, for a moment, she appeared as a young woman, deeply in love.

"Well, my dears," she said, "Mr. Lamb loved Jesus and served him all the days of his life. He was a wonderful husband and father. All of our children respected him and loved him dearly. His life was a demonstration of God's love and power."

I asked her when Mr. Lamb had gone home to be with the Lord and if he had been ill. She responded, "Well, my dear, one morning Mr. Lamb woke me up and held me very close and said, 'Honey, the Lord is calling me home. I want to pray for your protection.' He thanked the Lord for all the years He had given us together. He thanked the Lord for our children and our grandchildren. Mr. Lamb asked the Lord to watch over me and protect me in my remaining days on earth. He kissed me goodbye, laid his head back down on his pillow, closed his eyes and went home to be with Jesus." I was speechless. Shelly and I sat silently with Mrs. Lamb for a long while. It was beyond my comprehension to have such an intimate relationship with Jesus. There must have been total peace in Mr. Lamb's heart, demonstrating such an acceptance of the Lord's will for his life. How he had trusted the Lord!

What a deep impression was made on my life by a woman I barely knew and by a man I had never met. As Mrs. Lamb continued to speak, my heart was deeply touched with her love and reverence for her late husband. He was a true example of the saints of old, and I longed for such a faith as he had exhibited.

Shelly spoke at the evening church service and after the meeting Mrs. Lamb walked over to be with me. She put her hand on my shoulder and said, "It was so special to have you to my home today. We all did have such a wonderful time together. And, my dear, I will be waiting for you at the Eastern Gate." I was deeply affected by her words. I thanked Mrs. Lamb for having us to lunch and for opening her heart and life to us.

The following summer, Shelly was to be the guest speaker at Pastor Andrew's church. The church was so packed that there was standing room only. I remember sitting in the last row with my very dear friend, Ginny. She turned to me before the service and asked, "June, do you remember Mrs. Lamb, who had you to lunch last summer? She went home to be with the Lord, and her daughter is sitting in front of you."

My eyes filled up with tears as I remembered the special time we had shared together. My heart was so touched by the news of Mrs. Lamb's going home that I leaned forward and tapped her daughter on the shoulder and introduced myself.

I shared my experience with her mother and related her last words to me, "My dear, I will be waiting for you at the Eastern Gate." Her daughter wept, as she told me that she had wondered if her mother knew that she would soon be leaving this world. She was in good health and lived in perfect peace to the end. As Mrs. Lamb lived her life, so she entered into the world to come—in perfect peace.

Mrs. Lamb was not a missionary on a foreign field. She never wrote a book. She never formally taught a Bible study class. Her husband was not a minister by profession. She and her husband were simply dedicated to Jesus, to each other and to their children. She was a faithful wife, a beloved mother, grandmother and a faithful daughter of Zion.

⊸⟡⊷

During the trials and tribulations in life I'm reminded of Mrs. Lamb. She is an example of running the race to the finish line. May we desire to live such a prolific life, being unconditionally dedicated to the Lord Jesus, our Messiah. I look forward to the day I see Mrs. Lamb again. I know she will be waiting for me, just as she promised...

At The Eastern Gate

My message and my preaching
were not with wise and persuasive words,
but with a demonstration of the Spirit's power,
so that your faith might not rest on men's wisdom,
but on God's power.
I Corinthians 2:4, 5

BETTER THAN A SALAD BAR

...Feed me the food that is my portion...
Proverbs 30:8b

During our time in Connecticut, Shelly had spoken at a meeting on a Saturday night.

The meeting ended late and I was very hungry. There was a restaurant on the way to Ginny's house and I asked Shelly if we could stop. I wanted something from a salad bar.

Roselle was our waitress. She appeared to be in her late teens and was very personable. The children ordered and when it was my turn, I told her that I would like the salad bar. "Oh, I'm so sorry," she said, "The salad bar is closed."

I must confess that I was very disappointed; however, I told Roselle that there was something better than a salad bar. I asked her if she knew what that was and she replied, "A hamburger?" I told her it was better than a hamburger. She guessed again, "A tuna fish sandwich?" I told her better than a tuna fish sandwich. She asked me what that was. I told her—Jesus. Knowing He is alive and that He loves you is better than a salad bar. Her face flushed and she looked a bit shaken. She took the rest of our order.

Roselle told me many years later that when she went to place the order, she could hardly stand up. She had to lean against the water dispenser to keep herself from fainting. She felt the presence of the Lord, the power of God touching her life. She was undone!

After we finished eating, Roselle sat down with us at the table. She asked many questions about what it meant to know Jesus. She was brought up Catholic and never heard about having a personal relationship with the Lord. Shelly told her that, if she was interested in hearing more about the Lord, he would be speaking at a church in the morning and he gave her directions.

I don't remember what Shelly spoke that morning. However, at the end of his message, he asked if there was anyone who wanted to give their life to the Lord. He gave everyone the opportunity to come forward. It was so quiet in the sanctuary that you could have heard a pin drop. Shelly waited for awhile, and then one young woman came down the aisle trembling and weeping. It was Roselle. She bowed her knee and asked the Lord into her heart. She gave her life to Jesus.

Roselle visited with our family at Ginny's home. She told us that she would never be the same. She had chosen to serve the Lord all the days of her life. That has come to pass. Roselle married a strong believer and they have a large family. Jesus has been the heartbeat of her existence ever since she walked down the aisle and bowed her knee to the Lord, almost thirty years ago.

❧❧

When we serve the Lord there are no chance meetings. It was not by chance that we went to that particular restaurant. We need to be aware that God presents opportunities in the natural course of events, in our everyday affairs of life. Remember Roselle. Allow the Lord to unfold His plan through your life. There is nothing in this world that brings greater joy. Every moment of every day will become an adventure with Jesus.

He Is Alive

The steps of a good man are ordered by the LORD:
and he delighteth in his way.
Psalm 37:23

GOD'S PROTECTION

Honor (esteem and value as precious) your father and your
mother; this is the first commandment with a promise:
That all may be well with you
and that you may live long on the earth.
Ephesians 6:2, 3

One summer, we drove to Florida to visit my parents. While planning the activities for the day, they told us that they wanted to take us to the movie theater. Our children were not permitted to watch secular movies at that time. My parents were unaware of that, so we found ourselves in a dilemma. How were we to handle this situation? Shelly felt we should honor my parents by going to the theater, trusting that the Lord would protect the children if the film was inappropriate. We decided to go to the matinee and then to a restaurant for an early dinner.

The lights dimmed and, before we knew it, the movie was about to begin. Almost immediately, the family in the film had an argument and a curse word was spoken. I remember feeling my face flush, thinking how the children would reconcile our allowing them to watch and listen to what was on the screen.

At that very moment the screen went blank. The picture and the sound were gone. We heard a voice over the loud speaker telling us that they were working on the problem with the assurance that the film would resume shortly. As we sat in the dark theater for almost an hour, I thought, "Lord, You are awesome."

My parents were dumbfounded and asked each other repeatedly if they had ever experienced, seen or heard anything like this in their lives. And, our children marveled as they experienced the Hand of the Lord moving in the theatre.

Then the lights went on as a manager walked to the platform. He apologized for the inconvenience and thanked us for our patience. He could not explain why they were unable to get the projector to work properly. He gave us a choice of either going to another movie in that theater or getting a refund.

My parents could not believe what had happened. They asked what we preferred and we left the decision to them. They agreed to get a refund and have an earlier dinner.

While leaving the theater, they were trying to figure out what could have caused the problem. They thought perhaps a storm or an electrical outage. However, the sky was clear and we never did hear about an electrical problem.

My parents always remembered our experience at the theater that day. Scott, Dean and Suzi have also not forgotten what happened when we put our trust in the Lord by honoring their Grandma Claire and Grandpa Gus.

❧❧

We experienced God's protection and the Lord honored His Word. He also takes pleasure when children honor their parents. Try it and see.

Children Learn More By Example Than By Words

But, let all who take refuge in Thee be glad;
Let them ever sing for joy;
And mayest Thou shelter them,
That those who love Thy name
may exult in Thee.
Psalm 5:11

MR. PATTERSON

He was in the world, and the world was made through Him,
and the world did not know Him.
He came to His own, and those who were His own
did not receive Him.
John 1:10, 11

Patterson's was a fine men's clothing store owned by Mr. Patterson, a Jewish man in Bemidji. One day, Debbie and I were shopping at Patterson's when a lovely girl assisted us. She went to college in Colorado and was on her winter break. We had a long talk. I really liked her.

While walking to the car, Debbie asked me if I knew the girl I had spoken with was Mr. Patterson's daughter. My heart pounded as I told Debbie we should pray her into the Kingdom. We prayed that the Lord would send someone to tell her about Jesus when she returned to her college in Colorado.

Mr. Patterson knew we were Jewish believers. Shelly had talked with him about the Lord and, as a result, whenever Mr. Patterson saw either of us walking into his store, he would excuse himself and go to his office.

Several years later, we were scheduled to host a tour to Egypt and Israel with Art and Inger. The day before our flight, I realized that Shelly needed a belt, so I went to Bemidji to shop at Patterson's.

As I entered the store, Mr. Patterson greeted me warmly. He followed me around as I walked toward the belt rack and I wondered why he was being so friendly. He stood by the belt rack and initiated a conversation as I browsed through the belts. I told Mr. Patterson that we were leaving the following morning for the Middle East.

He stood by me at the rack as though we were old friends. It was so unlike him. I mustered up enough courage to ask, "Are you all right, Mr. Patterson?" He replied, "No, not really." He looked at me sheepishly, cleared his throat and asked, "Do you know what happened to you and Shelly?" I just stared at him for awhile, puzzled and I did not answer. He continued on, "Well, the same thing has happened to my daughter. She believes the same way you do."

I tried so hard to keep my composure. I could hardly believe what I said next, "Are you kidding, Mr. Patterson?" He looked so desperate when he responded, "No, I'm not kidding. My wife is deeply concerned about our daughter and she cannot understand what has happened. Would you consider visiting our home some time to help us understand what she believes?"

Still desperately trying to remain calm, I asked, "Would you like us to come to your home this evening?" Mr. Patterson looked confused, "But I thought you were leaving in the morning for the Middle East? What about packing? What about spending time with your children? Are you sure you will have the time to do everything you need to do before you leave?" I assured him that we would have the time we needed to accomplish everything. He phoned his wife to make the arrangements for our visit. We were to be at the Patterson home at seven that evening.

I skipped all the way to the car after leaving Mr. Patterson. Can you imagine a Jewish father and mother desiring to speak with us about Jesus? Unheard of!

I parked the car and hurried to Debbie's trailer to tell her the good news. My excitement greatly increased when Debbie responded, "Don't you remember, June, when we prayed for Mr. Patterson's daughter to come into the Kingdom years ago?" I had forgotten. The Lord knew that I never would have been able to contain myself as Mr. Patterson spoke to me, had I remembered our prayer.

Shelly was amazed when he heard what had happened. We decided to take the children out for dinner and then go to the Pattersons' home. When we arrived, we were warmly greeted and escorted into their living room. Almost immediately, they began asking questions: "How can you as Jews believe that Jesus is the Son of God? How can you believe the Messiah has already come? He is supposed to bring peace to the world and there is no peace. What caused you to believe in Jesus? Why did you change your religion?"

We both tried to answer their questions so they might have a better understanding of their daughter's faith. We trusted the Lord would enlighten their hearts as we spoke.

They seemed confounded when we stated we had not changed our religion. We explained that believing Jesus is the Messiah was the fulfillment of the promise to our people, which was written in the law, the psalms and the prophets. We shared how Jesus had given us an inner peace. When He comes again, we explained, He will then bring peace to the earth and fulfill His promise to our people Israel by restoring the Kingdom to them, Acts 1:6-8. We told them we are still Jewish because we believe Jesus is The King of the Jews. They listened intently, and seemed interested in what we were saying.

Mr. and Mrs. Patterson then shared with us their concerns for their daughter. She had met a young man at her college in Colorado, who was a Jewish believer, and she wanted to marry him. We tried to assure them of God's love for them and for their daughter. We encouraged them to talk to the Lord and He would teach them how to trust Him. The Pattersons' thanked us for coming and said that they now felt a greater measure of peace.

Their daughter did marry the young Jewish believer. He now works at Pattersons' clothing store. They have two beautiful children, and their faith has grown strong. They are a living testimony to the Jewish community in Bemidji.

శ్రీౡౝ

Sharing the Gospel and sowing seeds should become a way of life. Mr. Patterson's daughter could be your dentist, your teacher, your doctor or your friend. Prayer is also a way to sow a seed. Try it! There is no greater joy this side of heaven than the Lord's calling you to participate with Him to bring a soul into His Kingdom.

Marvelous Are Your Works

But as many as received Him,
to them He gave the right to become
children of God,
even to those who believe in His name.
John 1:12

THE MEDICAL STUDENTS

Forgive us our sins, for we also forgive everyone
who sins against us.
Luke 11:4a

I was thrilled with our visit to the Pattersons. Could our visit be a preview of the tour to Egypt and Israel? I had a deeper anticipation in my heart for our journey to the Middle East.

In the late seventies, the Lord gave me a burden for our kinsmen to be reconciled with our Arab cousins. The Scriptures make known that Abraham, the Lord's friend, loved Ishmael. The Lord's heart is broken over Ishmael, as well as over Israel. God's desire is for Arab and Jewish believers to proclaim the Lordship of Jesus together, with one voice.

And Abraham said to God,
"If only Ishmael might live under your blessing!"
Genesis 17: 18

The following verse declares God's covenant would be with Isaac:

Then God said,
"Yes, but your wife Sarah will bear you a son,
and you will call him Isaac.
I will establish my covenant with him as an everlasting covenant
for his descendants after him."
Genesis 17:19

My heart was broken for Hagar because of the circumstances of her life. I also could understand Sarah's dilemma in Genesis 21:9, 10. Today, more than five-thousand years later, we are observing the descendants of Hagar and Sarah, invariably at odds with one another.

Can real peace ever be established among our peoples? I believe that the true and lasting peace, *Salaam—Shalom*, will not come to our peoples until Jesus is recognized as the Lord of all and His Word becomes a way of life. Then our hearts will become one in the Messiah, who is the Savior of the world and the Prince of Peace.

It was in early spring of 1980, when Shelly and I hosted the tour with Art and Inger to Cairo, Egypt. Our tour bus was to be the first ever to cross the Suez Canal through the Sinai Desert into Israel.

One of the most memorable experiences occurred during our stay in Egypt. It was at a meeting with Christian medical students. We were graciously welcomed and everyone appeared to be very friendly. Art and Shelly sat in the front of the classroom facing all the students and I sat to the side with the guests from our tour.

Shelly and Art preached, and as Art was concluding, the still small voice of the Lord spoke to my heart: "The students are smiling, but they have hatred hidden in their hearts for the Jewish people. Read to them Genesis, Chapter 50 and tell them I desire to heal their bitterness and resentment."

I felt anxious with just the thought of speaking those words; I found myself arguing with the Lord about it. "Lord, could you please ask someone else to give that message? After all, I'm just a woman. Those words are piercing. Please ask someone else to speak for You."

I then heard Art say, "Someone in the room has a word from the Lord. Please speak it now." There was silence for several minutes. Art spoke up again, "Someone has a word from the Lord. Please speak it out now." It was as though the Lord pulled the words out of my mouth, and I heard myself voicing everything the Lord had asked me to say. As I finished, Art appeared to be a bit uneasy, understandably so. He asked if anyone else had something to say.

A holy hush filled the room until a female student, Merevet, stood to her feet. "I have something to say. I have not heard a word Art or Shelly has spoken. The reason being – I hate Jews. I have always hated Jews. And, I will always hate Jews." The air became so thick in the room, you could have cut it with a knife. The smile on every student's face faded away.

Art cleared his throat, and he then shared his burden for reconciliation between the German and the Jew. Art continued, "Perhaps the Lord is desirous of a demonstration of forgiveness here today, between the Arab and the Jew." A black woman from our tour group spoke about her previous hatred for white people. Her heart had been filled with bitterness and hurts, until Jesus healed her.

Art said, "It's time for us to pray." While we were praying, I asked the Lord, "May I please go to Merevet?" The Lord said, "No." I asked again, "Please, Lord, may I go to Merevet?" Again the Lord said, "No." The third time I asked Him if I could go to her He told me, "No. She needs to come to you."

As He spoke, I felt arms around my shoulders and someone's tears running down my neck. I turned and saw Merevet looking into my eyes, "Can you please forgive me for hating your people?" I wept as I replied, "Yes. I forgive you. Can you forgive me and forgive my people for the pain we have caused your people?" "Yes, yes, I forgive you," she sobbed as we embraced each other, weeping together.

Suddenly, Merevet drew back with a startled expression, "I don't hate you anymore. I don't hate Jews anymore." We cried together as we thanked the Lord for demonstrating His healing power.

The male students were somber as they brought a basin of water and towels to the front of the room. Weeping, they knelt down and washed Art and Shelly's feet. They asked forgiveness for resenting Israel and the Jewish people. They all wept together.

Merevet drove me to a Coptic Church to speak with the women. I told her how I had wanted to comfort her at the meeting and had asked the Lord three times to let me go to her, but each time He had refused. She appeared shocked. "You are not going to believe this," she said. "I asked the Lord three times to bring you to me. But He told me, No. I needed to go to you."

What an example this was to me of the healing and deliverance that comes when one asks or extends forgiveness.

For if you forgive people their trespasses—
that is, their reckless and willful sins, leaving them,
letting them go and giving up resentment—
your heavenly Father will also forgive you.

But if you do not forgive others their trespasses—
their reckless and willful sins, leaving them,
letting them go, and giving up resentment—
neither will your Father forgive you your trespasses.
Matthew 6:14, 15

ৰ৵৵

Do you have bitterness or resentment in your heart against anyone? Are you hurt? Are you jealous? Do you feel cheated or misused? Ask the Lord to restore your soul. Ask Him what you can do to see victory come and whatsoever He says to you, do it. Just as the Lord surprised Merevet by putting love in her heart for the Jewish people, He will surprise you with the grace to overcome. And He surprised me, too!

Show Me My Heart, O LORD

So, as the Holy Spirit says:
"Today, if you hear his voice,
do not harden your hearts..."
Hebrews 3:7, 8a

The Cry of My Heart

Reconciliation dear Lord Reconciliation
Restore Your family Arab and Jew
Bring love dear Lord bring love
So we might worship You the Holy One
Together

Pain and hurt rejection to name a few
Are areas of need to be healed by You
Help us Lord to see You as Messiah
To bring wholeness and holiness to us all
Together

Wash our feet change our minds
To see in us the Eternal Hope abide
Israel Palestine to agree with You
To see Your coming in the clouds
Together

In Your Spirit make us One
In Your Spirit to see Your Son
United in prayer and worship
Of the God of Abraham
Together

June Volk

PRAYER CHANGES THINGS

Pray without ceasing.
I Thessalonians 5:17

Prayer is entering into a deep place of communion with the Living God. Prayer is more than asking for something that we desire. There is quite a difference between saying our prayers or entering into a life of prayer. I'm reminded of a song Keith Green wrote, "Make My Life A Prayer To You." The question is, "Has your life become a prayer to the Lord?"

Prayer had been burned deep within my heart. I found myself praying without ceasing because I was aware of my desperate need of God. As believers, we have become proficient in saying our prayers, while all along the Lord has been waiting for our lives to become a prayer to Him. It is possible for our attitudes to be altered while going about our daily routine in prayer. In reality, prayer changes people.

Brother Lawrence discovered this truth as he desired to live consistently in the presence of God. When Brother Lawrence entered the monastery, he pictured himself in solemn prayer and separation from the world with all its entanglements. Was he ever surprised when he discovered that scrubbing pots and pans would be his daily chore. It was during those hours of scrubbing that his life changed, as he practiced being in the presence of God. He set an example for us in the book, *The Practice of the Presence of God.* He prayed without ceasing.

You might be thinking, "But I'm not a monk. I live in the real world. I'm just an ordinary person who wants to get closer to Jesus."

Since I'm just an ordinary person also, housewife, mother and grandmother, I would like to encourage you that throughout your day, while engaged in your ordinary chores, your life can be changed. You also can be used in extra ordinary ways, as you practice being in the presence of God while you pray without ceasing.

MATTHEW

During our first year on the farm, I started cooking the *Shabbat* meals in our trailer rather than down at camp. I had realized that as the *Shabbat* meal was cooking, I could also do my weekly cleaning.

One Friday morning, while cleaning the bathroom, I could not stop thinking about our dear brother and friend, Matthew. I was so concerned for him that I stopped what I was doing, prostrated myself on the floor and prayed for a very long time.

Several months later, Shelly and I saw Matthew in Kansas City. I asked if anything unusual had happened on a Friday morning during the past few months. He was startled and wanted to know why I asked. I told him about the urgency in my spirit to pray and how I had prayed for a long while, until I had peace.

"That is very interesting," Matthew said. "One Friday morning, I was driving with a friend in my little car. A huge truck hit us as I was making a turn. We got out of the car traumatized. We were in shock! My car was crushed, totaled, and miraculously, we did not have a scratch on us."

✥

Follow through with what you believe to be the leading of the Holy Spirit and...

Pray without ceasing
I Thessalonians 5:17

GRAYCE

One morning, as I was going about my daily chores, the thought of Grayce would not leave me. After praying for her for a long while, I still had unrest, so I phoned. Gracye was unable to walk because of terrible back pain. She had been thrown from a horse many years before and suffered from recurring back problems. The doctors wanted to operate and her prognosis was not good. They feared she might never walk again. I encouraged her to pray with her husband, Jack, for wisdom and to wait on their decision until they both had peace.

Blessed is the man who trusts in the LORD
And whose trust is the LORD.
Jeremiah 17:7

Grayce called back to let me know that when I had phoned, Jack was in the barn crying out to the Lord. He had unrest about surgery yet did not want to upset her by asking Gracye to wait for the Lord to raise her up. He took her feelings into consideration, realizing that she was the one with chronic back pain.

When Jack returned from the barn and heard I had phoned, he wept. He told Gracye about his unrest and they prayed together. The timing of my call gave Gracye the faith to wait on the Lord with peace in her heart. That was over twenty-two years ago, and the last time we spoke to Grayce, she was still walking without pain.

༄༅

Follow through with what you believe to be the leading of the Holy Spirit and...

Pray without ceasing.
I Thessalonians 5:17

ANDY

While cooking, Andy came strongly to mind, so I asked Shelly if we could pray for him. Andy was a Jewish friend who was not a believer, although we had shared our faith with him many times. We prayed for a long time until we both felt peace.

I wrote Andy to ask if anything unusual had happened to him. I noted the time and date that we prayed. His response amazed me.

Andy and his friends had rented a boat that day. A storm had come up unexpectedly and the rudder of the boat cracked at the exact time we had prayed. Without a rudder, it was impossible to steer the boat, so they were being tossed aimlessly to and fro. They all questioned if they would survive the storm. Somehow, the boat made it to shore without any casualties. Andy and his friends considered themselves lucky to be alive.

He was surprised when I wrote that we had prayed for him. Andy and his friends now had to consider the intervention of God sparing their lives through prayer. May this experience be an ingredient for their ultimate salvation.

᠊ᡃᠥᢇᠣ᠊

Follow through with what you believe to be the leading of the Holy Spirit and...

Pray without ceasing.
I Thessalonians 5:17

SCOTT, DEAN & SUZI'S
WATER BAPTISMS

Fulfill your promise to your servant, so that you may be feared.
Psalm 119:38

During our first visit to Minnesota in 1975, Scott was together with Shelly, Paul, Arthur and Phil on the upper level of the barn when he asked them to pray for him. They all knelt and when they started to pray, Shelly saw an angel hovering over the barn. He could hardly believe his eyes.

Inger and I were cooking when Scott walked into the farmhouse. I looked at his glowing countenance and asked him if he had been touched by the Lord. Scott seemed surprised by my question. I explained that as he walked through the door, I was aware that he no longer belonged to me, but that he belonged to the Lord.

It was the first time that I had an understanding of what my mother had tried to express to me after I came to faith in Jesus. She told me that I was no longer her daughter; she realized that something had changed. Scott then told me what had happened to him in the barn and told me that he needed to be baptized.

When Dean overheard what Scott told me, he also wanted to be baptized. Because of his age and the significance of such a decision, Arthur tried to encourage Dean to wait. Phil also tried to dissuade him and after much dialogue, Arthur asked Dean why he wanted to be baptized. Dean looked Arthur straight in the eye and boldly declared, because Jesus wanted him to be baptized. Without hesitation, Arthur told Dean to put on his bathing suit. Dean was so thrilled to be given the opportunity to be baptized that he ran to get his bathing suit.

We filled up the bathtub, and all huddled close together in that tiny space as our boys went into the waters of baptism. Scott was ten years old and Dean was one month shy of turning nine. The Lord had revealed Himself to Shelly and brought him through the waters of baptism. Now, He had brought Scott and Dean to that same place of dedication. That day I told the Lord I looked forward to when He would call Suzi to the waters of baptism.

Many summers passed before Suzi heard the call. One evening, at a youth meeting at Camp Dominion, the presence of God was so powerful that Suzi wept. She asked the Lord if there was anything more that He desired for her. It was then that Suzi heard the still small voice of the Lord calling her to the waters of baptism.

As I stood on the dock of Steamboat Lake at Camp Dominion that day, the sunlight sparkled on the waters. Suzi, my little girl, was now tall enough to stand in the waters about fifteen feet from the dock. I could hardly believe the day had arrived that Suzi was getting baptized. Tears rolled down my cheeks, as Shelly and Arthur lifted Suzi from the waters of baptism. Thank you, Lord, Suzi is completely Yours.

The Lord had promised me that one day my family would know Him and serve Him. I realize after many years of serving the Lord that when God promises something, He keeps His promise even if we doubt.

Baptism is very foreign to Jewish people. However, it is the most Jewish thing you can do. To be buried with the Messiah into His death and to be raised up into newness of life is a blessing and demonstration of our commitment and love to Jesus. I feel privileged to share this testimony of how Jesus called our children to the waters of baptism.

While editing this vignette, we received a phone call from Suzi telling us that her children were entering into the waters of baptism the following day. All of our grandchildren have now been baptized; they have all dedicated their lives to Jesus. Thank You, Lord.

≪⌘≫

Have you entrusted your loved ones to the Lord? Trust God and believe in His promises without fear. He will answer you – you can be sure of it. Have you heard God calling you to enter the waters of baptism? Be blessed and know that you too can be buried with Jesus and be raised up to newness of life, in Him, from the book of Romans, Chapter 6. He is waiting for you, do not delay.

Believe His Promises Without Fear

For all the promises of God in him are yea,
and in him Amen,
unto the glory of God by us.
II Corinthians 1:20

When God made his promise to Abraham,
since there was no one greater for him to swear by,
he swore by himself, saying,
"I will surely bless you and give you many descendants."
And so after waiting patiently,
Abraham received what was promised.
Hebrews 6:13 - 15

ONE MORE BEAT

He who spares the rod hates his son,
but he who loves him is careful to discipline him.
Proverbs 13:24

While pregnant with Dean, my stomach was bruised from his kicking. I thought that he would one day be a drummer. As a child, his hands and feet moved constantly, he was always keeping the beat. When Dean was a teenager, he bought a drum starter set with money that had been given to him. Dean had prayed for the drums.

Our trailer was very small and when Dean practiced his drums, the vibrations made it seem even smaller. He loved to worship the Lord on his drums.

Our trailer was overflowing with guests one evening as Dean was practicing on his drums in his bedroom. I was preparing the meal and couldn't hear a word anyone was speaking, there was so much noise.

I called out to Dean and asked him to please play a little softer. A short time later, I called out again and asked him to please stop playing. I could not believe that Dean did not obey me. I called out again that if I heard One More Beat, I would have to spank him. In the following moment, I heard a soft *chshshsh*.

I told Dean that when I finished sautéing the onions and green peppers, I would be coming into his room with the wooden spoon and to prepare himself for a spanking. I moved the onions and green peppers from the burner and excused myself from our guests.

Dean was on his bed pouting with his arms folded across his chest. I tried to be gentle with him and explained that I had warned him to stop playing the drums. He looked up at me with his sweet face and sparkling eyes and with the most sincere expression said, "But Mom, I just had One More Beat." I explained to Dean that if he could not obey my voice that was audible, how could he learn to obey the still small voice of the Lord when he grew up and was on his own.

I asked Dean if he understood that I loved him, and he assured me he knew that I did. I also wanted to know if he had prepared his heart for his spanking. He asked me to please wait one second as he pulled two small pillows out from the back of his jeans. He looked at me earnestly and said, "Okay, Mom, I'm ready."

Dean always brought laughter to my heart. He had a way about him; he was such a prankster. But somehow, the Lord had broken through to his heart with the seriousness of his disobedience. I must confess that amazed me. By the goodness of God, Dean was led to repentance.

⊰⊱

May you come to understand the love of God and that He desires to train you up to be His son or daughter. It can be quite painful. However, His correction results in your turning from your own ways to His ways.

God's Discipline Is Always For Your Good

Although he was a son,
he learned obedience from what he suffered...
Hebrews 5:8a

A SIP OF SODA

Therefore we do not lose heart.
Though outwardly we are wasting away,
yet inwardly we are being renewed day by day.
II Corinthians 4:16

Shelly was scheduled to meet with the leadership of a church in New England to help resolve their differences. The evening before their meeting, we met with Andy for dinner, the young man in the boat incident. When Shelly took a sip of soda, a sharp knife like pain struck him in his abdomen. As the evening progressed, the pain worsened.

The following morning, Shelly's coloring was a pale green and he appeared to have dropped some weight. An elder of the church phoned a close friend who was a doctor. When Shelly described his pain, the doctor told him that he had a surgical abdomen. He strongly suggested that we get to the hospital immediately.

The doctor was waiting when we arrived. Shelly had a series of tests that indicated a possible problem with his pancreas. The doctor wanted to admit him to the hospital. Shelly told him that he needed to be at a meeting that evening, and would admit himself afterward.

It was revealed at the meeting with the church leaders, that their problems were very complicated. Shelly prayed that the Lord would clarify the problem and bring resolve. Shelly then admitted himself into the hospital and was sent to a surgical floor.

By the following afternoon, I was in turmoil over Shelly remaining in the hospital. They had given him a lower GI series and he was on intravenous fluids. I met his doctor in the hallway and asked if he had identified the problem. He explained that the symptoms weren't adding up and was puzzled over the cause and location of the pain. This was very similar to what Shelly had experienced the night before at the meeting with the pastor and elders—nothing added up!

I shared my unrest with Shelly about his remaining in the hospital. He looked up at me as if I was crazy and replied, "The pain is in my stomach not yours." His doctor entered the room and told Shelly that he wanted to perform exploratory surgery. Shelly told his doctor that he wanted to be discharged. I was shocked and his doctor appeared very alarmed.

Shelly explained he was a preacher and was scheduled to speak at different churches in upstate New York. He felt obligated to keep those appointments. His doctor warned him that he would never make upstate New York with the pain he was experiencing.

After much discussion, his doctor sighed and stated that it was a free country. If he wanted to be discharged, he couldn't stop him. He told us to phone him at the hospital in upstate New York, and he would forward his records. He ordered the nurse to remove the intravenous and prepare Shelly to be discharged.

Shelly's pain was so intense that he could barely walk. He was doubled over holding his stomach. I was so frightened as thoughts raced through my mind: Maybe my unrest was my own fear and not the Holy Spirit. Maybe Shelly should have the surgery. Maybe …

As we entered the elevator, a nurse was running down the hall panicking as she cried out after us, "Mr. Volk, Mr. Volk, you can't leave the hospital. This is the surgical floor!" She was in shock as the elevator doors closed in front of us.

Shelly went directly to bed when we got to the apartment, and I phoned our friends in Kingston, New York. I explained the situation we were in and asked them to please pray for wisdom. Several hours passed before they phoned back. Their advice was that if Shelly could do nothing more regarding the problem with the church leaders, we should leave the city immediately. And so we did.

In Kingston, Shelly went directly to bed. That evening, he preached at church and met with the leadership. Our next destination was Brockport, several hours away. Shelly did keep his speaking engagements and was not admitted to the hospital in upstate New York. A few weeks later we arrived back home to Minnesota safely.

However, his pain was more severe and Shelly had dropped more weight. His coloring was somewhere between pale green and yellow. His former secretary, Catherine, telephoned to inform us that a Jewish salesman, who had worked in Shelly's office, had been diagnosed with cancer of the pancreas and was given three months to live. Shelly's color worsened!

Many months later, I accompanied Shelly on a ministry trip to Iowa. One morning about five-o'clock, fear overwhelmed me. I cried out to the Lord, that if He was calling Shelly home, to please give us and the children the grace to bear it. I released Shelly into His safekeeping and prayed that if this was an attack from Satan, the Lord would rebuke him. I also asked for a sign that if Shelly was going to live, five pounds would be added to his countenance later on that morning. I was then able to sleep with deep peace in my heart.

At about ten-o'clock that morning, I found Shelly sitting in a recliner. It looked as though five pounds had been added to his countenance. His face shone and his coloring was back to normal. My heart rejoiced within me; I could hardly believe my eyes. I told Shelly he looked healthier and asked him what had happened.

He told me that about six-o'clock that morning he got on his knees and prayed, "God if you are calling me home, please give us and the children the grace to bear it." He committed his soul into the Lord's safekeeping. He then told Satan he was bound and let him know he had no part with him. Shelly said he felt better than he had in months. Shelly was healed, and we prayed the identical prayer!

∽⌒∾

Are you going through a deep trial or affliction? Going to doctors or having surgery is not the issue. God is able to work through doctors or surgery. Yielding your will to God is the heart of the matter. Don't give into your fears. Remember, what started with a sip of soda ended with a taste of His touch.

Cry out to God—Obey His Voice—Trust Him And Wait For His Victory To Come

Taste and see that the LORD is good;
blessed is the man who takes refuge in him.
Psalm 34:8

A PICKLE

But if we walk in the light as He Himself is in the light,
we have fellowship with one another,
and the blood of Jesus His Son cleanses us from all sin.
1 John 1:7

The challenges of living in a Christian community were new every morning, as were God's mercies. The Lord taught me so many lessons about my heart for which I'm eternally grateful. This is one of those lessons learned from a pickle.

Every summer when we harvested our crops, we canned or froze them for the winter. We always had an abundance of cucumbers that we pickled. Mark and Donna made the best sour pickles you ever tasted. We had a common food house where all the food was stored, and their pickles were the first to disappear off the shelves.

Our common food supplies brought many trials to the women in the community. We learned to trust the Lord for enough food for our individual families, without hoarding. I could write a book about the lessons learned. They ranged from asking the Lord what He was trying to teach me to "How could she?"

One day, Mark knocked on our door and asked if I had any of his pickles. He had checked the food house and every jar of his recipe was gone. I told him that we didn't have any of his pickles. Soon after he left, I opened the refrigerator and there was a pickle in one of his jars sitting on a shelf. Instead of taking the pickle to Mark's trailer and giving it to him, I threw it in the garbage. Needless to say, that was a crazy thing to do. However, the evidence of a pickle was gone.

At least I did not eat the pickle, so I didn't have to feel guilty. Right? Wrong! I felt so guilty that I was not honest with Mark, that a pickle was all I could think about. I lost sleep over the pickle cover-up. Really, it might seem absurd or humorous, but I was troubled. I honestly don't remember how long I lived with the feeling of guilt. I was ashamed to confess what I had done. What a pickle I was in!

One afternoon, I mustered up enough courage to take the long walk to the garage where Mark worked. He was busy fixing a car when I asked if I could talk with him. He told me to wait a minute and I remember that that minute seemed like forever.

My heart started to pound as Mark walked toward me. He asked what he could do for me, and I looked up into his eyes and cried. My voice was cracking terribly. I told him I needed to ask his forgiveness and I was too embarrassed to tell him why.

I continued on and asked if he remembered coming to my trailer for his pickles. He said he remembered. He also remembered that I had told him I didn't have any pickles. I explained that when I opened the refrigerator there was a pickle in one of his jars sitting on a shelf. I was too embarrassed to tell him, so I threw it in the garbage.

I asked him to please forgive me. I shared how sorry I was for what had happened. Mark laughed and assured me that all was well and I was forgiven.

I asked Mark to pray for me so that I would never conceal the truth again. Mark prayed and the peace of God returned to my heart.

ಊಐ

May the story of a pickle remain as near to your heart as it has to mine. Never allow yourself to be involved in a cover-up.

Do Not Allow Yourself To Get Caught In A Pickle

He who conceals his sins does not prosper,
but whoever confesses and renounces them finds mercy.
Proverbs 28:13

Therefore confess your sins to each other and
pray for each other so that you may be healed.
The prayer of a righteous man is powerful and effective.
James 5:16

GRANDMA RUTH

Charm is deceptive, and beauty is fleeting;
but a woman who fears the LORD is to be praised.
Give her the reward she has earned,
and let her works bring her praise at the city gate.
Proverbs 31:30, 31

Grandma Ruth had known Jesus for more than fifty years before she received her call into His service. She was seventy years old.

She was being rushed into the operating room when she overheard a doctor telling her daughters they would do everything they could to save her life, but it did not look promising. Ruth was hemorrhaging. It was then that she heard God's call. He told her that she would not die but live and proclaim His Name to many nations.

Ruth recovered quickly. A friend phoned about a mission needing someone to live on the Chippewa Indian Reservation, in the northern woods of Minnesota. Because Ruth remembered the Word that she would proclaim God's Name to many nations, and since the Native American people are made up of many nations, she decided to visit the mission.

The Indian culture is matriarchal, so there is a deep respect for grandmothers. Ruth lived among the Chippewa people and served them for fourteen years. Her passion for the Lord brought Indian leaders as well as many women and children to Jesus. She also loved the Word of God and cherished it deep within her heart.

Grandma Ruth was a physically strong woman. She drew water from a lake daily, which was a good distance, and hauled it in a bucket to her home. She was a wonderful homemaker and loved to bake bread. Grandma Ruth also made the most delicious sweet rolls from scratch, the best you ever tasted. She planted and tended her own vegetable garden and canned her own food. Grandma Ruth taught the Indian women how to preserve food for their long winters.

She was eighty-four when she came to live with us on the farm. Grandma Ruth loved flowers. She planted her own flowerbeds and cared for them nobly. I can still picture her bending over, weeding her flower garden. She also helped weed the community vegetable garden, and her unyielding stamina put all the young women to shame.

She never forgot her call to the Indian nation and they never forgot her. Her trailer was always filled with friends, young and old from the reservation. Ruth was a great prayer warrior. I remember many prayer meetings on the reservation that lasted till the wee hours of the morning. A strong fellowship of believers was raised up in Red Lake through prayer, during a time of war on the Red Lake Reservation. Ruth was there praying.

At the age of ninety, Grandma Ruth went to a nursing home in Minneapolis. Her memory was failing and she had congenital heart failure. Her heart was also broken, feeling rejected by her daughters. Grandma Ruth did not want to grow bitter or resentful. Even with her inner struggles, her countenance remained bright.

Some time passed before I saw Grandma Ruth again. She was sitting in the waiting room with other residents when we arrived. She took my hands in hers and rubbed them as she always had. I asked her if she knew me and she shook her head no. She did not remember any of us who were visiting.

Her long white hair that was once neatly fixed in a bun was untended. She had on the same dress that once was starched and clean; now it was spotted and wrinkled. She had lost her glasses and her teeth were gone as well. Tears rolled down my cheeks as I remembered how Grandma Ruth had kept herself and now…

Nevertheless, when we read from the Scriptures, she completed the verses. The Word had been planted in her heart. When we sang praise songs that she once loved, Grandma Ruth sang along and did not miss a word.

As we were about to leave, she tried to stand up and walk with us. Everyone in the waiting room gasped and shouted – NO! Only then did we realize to what extent Grandma Ruth was incapacitated. She had not walked for almost a year. We hugged and kissed her good-bye. We all knew it was the last time we would see Grandma Ruth this side of heaven.

I was reminded on that last visit with Grandma Ruth that she had given me a written message for my birthday when I turned forty. It touched my heart so deeply I had taped it on the inside of my kitchen cabinet door. On one of our visits to the farm many years later, I found the note still taped on the door. It read:

Toil on Sister June—
Remember He Who Is Faithful In Little
—Is Faithful In Much

The testimony of Jesus within never fades away. Grandma Ruth's heart was filled with the life of Jesus and His Word. Although everything natural was fading away, her spirit was as alive and free as the first day I had met her.

❦

Don't lose heart. Remember, Grandma Ruth was seventy when she heard the call. What a mission! We are never too old to fulfill the purposes of God that He has planned for us. It is always encouraging for me to think of the great cloud of witnesses in heaven cheering us on. I believe that Grandma Ruth is among them, waiting for us to join her.

Listen For His Call—And Obey His Leading

Therefore we do not lose heart.
Though outwardly we are wasting away,
yet inwardly we are being renewed day by day.
For our light and momentary troubles are achieving for us
an eternal glory that far outweighs them all.
So we fix our eyes not on what is seen,
but on what is unseen.
For what is seen is temporary,
but what is unseen is eternal.
II Corinthians 4:16-18

SWEET ROLLS

Or do you show contempt for the riches
of his kindness, tolerance and patience,
not realizing that God's kindness
leads you toward repentance?
Romans 2:4

In every meaningful relationship there are times of conflict. Even with the Lord, there are seasons when Jesus might bid us to be with Him and share in the fellowship of His suffering, and our old nature might rise up to resist. Such a conflict once arose between Shelly and me. I am thankful that the details of why I was so upset are erased from my memory. Having a natural ability for details I hope it encourages you, as it has me, that the Lord is able to heal you and cause you to forget.

I was so upset that I took my bedding into the living room to sleep on the couch. I cried for a long while and told the Lord that I was finished with Shelly, even if it meant losing my salvation. Even if I never heard His voice again or never saw Him face to face, I was not going to allow myself to be hurt or feel so irreparable again. I cried for hours until I fell asleep.

I was awakened by a persistent knocking on my door. I was embarrassed that I had slept on the couch, so I picked up the bedding and threw it into our bedroom. I asked quietly who it was, when I heard Grandma Ruth asking me to please open the door. I was surprised to see her standing in the freezing cold, holding a tray covered with a kitchen towel. I asked her why she had come out at six o'clock that cold winter morning.

She told me that she couldn't sleep, so she got out of bed and tried to pray. Her spirit remained disturbed, until she heard the voice of the Lord telling her to bake sweet rolls and bring them to me, first thing in the morning.

Grandma Ruth was eighty-seven and was up all night baking me sweet rolls. I felt ashamed. It was too much for me to handle because I deserved a spanking for my attitude. Why would the Lord show me so much mercy? And to add to my shame, Grandma Ruth had a message for me from the Lord: Jesus loves you very much.

Sweet rolls and a message that Jesus loved me, can you even imagine such a God? I had told Jesus for all practical purposes, I was finished with Him. To this day, such love amazes me. While I was filled with bitterness, He demonstrated His sweetness. He really is altogether different than we are. He broke my heart with His goodness and His love.

I repented and asked the Lord to forgive me. I asked Him to please help me to never say the words *I am finished* again. The Lord was not finished with me. Why should I ever be finished with Shelly or anyone else? Why should I ever come close to losing my communion with the Lord again? Then I remembered, when Jesus said, *it is finished,* it cost Him His life.

∽᙮᠊

We serve a living God. He is the One who cares about every detail of your life. Do not be afraid to be honest with Him. Let the Lord break your heart as He broke mine, with His mercy and His love.

His Mercies Are New Every Morning

Little children,
let us not love with word or with tongue,
but in deed and truth.
I John 3:18

DR. STUBBINS

That at the name of Jesus every knee should bow,
of things in heaven, and things in earth, and things
under the earth...
Philippians 2:10

While pregnant with Dean, I had my four front teeth capped, because I was fearful of having a filling replaced between my two front teeth.

About twelve years later, one of the center front caps split in half. Shelly and I were in the Twin Cities with close friends and they set up an appointment with their dentist. He put on a temporary cap and told me to see my dentist when I returned home. Little did he know, we did not have a dentist nor did we have the money to go to one. The temporary cap lasted for several years.

While eating a bagel one morning, the cap split in half in the same spot. I bought non-toxic glue and with Shelly's assistance, we glued the cap together. A short time passed when the cap split in the same place, but this time the problem increased because I could not find the other half. I cannot tell you what bothered me more, the terrible pain or my appearance. The situation was so awful, I finally phoned the dentist in Bemidji who had been highly recommended by the dentist in Minneapolis. That is how I met Dr. Stubbins.

His nurse was so kind when I phoned that she set up an appointment that same day. But how can I have the cap replaced without money? When I arrived at the office, I was impressed at how modern and clean it was. Dr. Stubbins was very personable. As he looked in my mouth, he tried to encourage me to cap both front teeth, not just the one. He told me that it would be very difficult to match the color of my other cap. I asked him how much it would cost and he told me $500.

But $500 could have been $5 million to me at that time. I swallowed hard and asked Dr. Stubbins to please put on a temporary cap. His response was so kind. He assured me that I could pay the bill at my own pace. I told him that we didn't believe in owing money because we lived by faith. I said that if he wanted to trust Jesus for the money, he could cap my teeth. I honestly thought that would cause him to put a temporary cap on my tooth.

Was I ever wrong! He looked me right in the eye and said, "I want to trust Jesus for the money." He immediately started the preparatory work for the two caps, as I sat with my mouth wide open, speechless. After he completed the work for that visit, he asked me to meet him in his private office. He instructed his assistant to set up a special file for me. I was not to be billed for his services. He told her to be sure I never received a late payment notice. And he told me, I was not to worry because he was trusting Jesus for the funds.

He wanted to know what I meant when I said that we live by faith. Dr. Stubbins heard about our call, patted me on the head and walked out of his office. I had found a new friend in Dr. Stubbins.

At our prayer meeting the following morning, I shared what had happened. I asked everyone to please pray for a release of the funds; I did not want to shame the Name of the Lord. About three days later, I received a letter from a woman we knew in upstate New York. As she was praying, she saw my face; my name was placed deep in her heart. She wrote that she wanted to take $500 out of her bank account and send it to me, but she felt her husband would not understand. So instead, she sent a $50 check as a love gift. The Lord put my heart at ease. He was going to pay my dental bill.

I told everyone about Dr. Stubbins and encouraged them to use him as their dentist. I received a thank you card from his office about a year later. It said that in all the years he had practiced dentistry, he had never received as many patients from one person's referral.

Dr. Stubbins blessed me and the Lord returned the blessing to him, pressed down and running over.

Within one year, the $500 was paid. As I received checks, dollar bills or coins, I would take them to his office. His receptionist, who kept his books, asked what it was about me because every time I gave her my payments, she would get chills all over her body. She never had experienced anything like that in her life.

Both Shelly and Dean had dental work done. Dr. Stubbins was also an orthodontist. Scott and Suzi needed braces. The same rule of payment was followed for our family and the Lord provided for all services rendered. Let your heart take courage, the Lord knows your every need. I can remember sending Dr. Stubbins the last payment for Suzi's braces from Phoenix, Arizona with a smile on my face.

∽❧

The Lord's greatest desire is to meet you and bless you, as you learn to put your trust in Him. He will surprise you as He did me. He is a faithful loving Father to all of His children.

Trust Him—Call Out To Him
He Will Never Fail You

Until now you have not asked anything in my name.
Ask and you will receive, and your joy will be complete.
John 16:24

SAGASAGAY

He rescues and he saves;
he performs signs and wonders in the heavens and on the earth.
Daniel 6:27a

While at a church service in Cass Lake, I was surprised when someone came to tell me that I had a phone call. Who would be calling me at church and why?

Anna, my dear sister and friend, was in labor and her water had just broken. Her husband, Willie Atkinson, who was a Chippewa Indian, phoned to let me know that they were waiting for me to come to deliver their baby. Before I had a chance to respond, Willie had hung up.

I could not phone him back, since he did not have a phone in his house. This was Anna's second baby and I realized it was possible for her to deliver quickly. Over the years, I had been with many women during their labor, but I had never been called to deliver a baby. A midwife or nurse was always present.

Willie had built a house in the middle of the woods, but I had no idea where. I also knew that they did not have running water or electricity and the temperature that day was about thirty below zero.

I hurried back to my seat, obviously shaken up by the call. My friend Ginny was visiting during her winter-break from nursing school. She wanted to know if there was a problem. I asked her to put on her coat because she was coming with me to deliver a baby. Her eyes opened wide as she said emphatically, "Oh no, I'm not!"

I leaned over to Jeff who had been to Willie's house. I asked him to please direct us, because Anna was in labor. Jeff quickly put on his jacket while Ginny reluctantly walked with us to the car.

My heart was beating faster than usual as thoughts were racing through my head. Jeff had lived on a farm in Argentina and had experience delivering animals. If we were desperate, he might be able to assist us. However, deep within my heart, I truly hoped that the midwife would be at the house before we arrived.

Ginny looked stunned as she picked up a book from the kitchen table, not quite believing her eyes. She had prayed that if she were to have part in this birth, her exact nursing book was to be on the kitchen table, and there it was. She was now completely with me for which I was grateful, because I really needed her help.

Willie and Anna had just returned from the Twin Cities, so they had made no preparations for the delivery. We had need of: clean sheets, towels, plastic to cover the bedding, an aspirator, scissors, string to tie the cord, clean cloths, etc...

According to the nursing textbook, we could use paper bags to sterilize in a wood stove. What good was the information without the paper bags and no telephone? We really needed help.

To complicate matters, Anna was nervous about having the baby at home. Anna had asked Willie to please take her to the hospital, but Willie called me instead.

We prayed for the Lord to send someone to get the supplies we needed. We asked the Lord to please give peace to Anna about having the baby at home, or to change Willie's heart about taking her to the hospital. Anna seemed to calm down after we prayed.

We heard knocking at the door. It was a neighbor wanting to know if we were in need of anything. Ginny had made a list of items needed and the neighbor did the shopping.

Ginny seemed calmer, having her nursing book that gave the details about the birthing procedure. The neighbor returned quickly with everything on the list. We began to sterilize by taking snow from the window ledges and filling a bowl. We placed the bowl with the snow on the bottom shelf of the oven in the wood stove.

The melted snow prevented the paper bags, filled with the items, from burning. We filled a pot with snow and put it on top of the wood stove to melt and brought it to a boil for the scissors, string, aspirator, etc. As we worked to prepare everything for the birth, the Lord spoke to me: "And, where was I born? How sterile was the barn? Who is the giver and taker of life? If a baby is in My hands, I can take care of everything. The baby will be safe."

We made up the bed with the clean sheets and covered the bedding with plastic. Everything was prepared for the birth, so I went upstairs to sit by Anna's side. She told me that she felt to push, but she was so calm and quiet it seemed too soon. She asked me to please check her progress. The head of the baby was crowning. Time to push!

In a flash, Willie, Jeff and Gea, their five-year-old son, came running up the stairs. Ginny was waiting to catch the baby. In two pushes, out came their beautiful baby daughter, Sagasagay (Light in the Midst of the Trees).

I put Sagasagay on Anna's stomach and we all lifted our arms in high praise to the Lord. What a special moment in light of eternity. I tied the umbilical cord with string and Willie cut it.

Ginny called me into another room, where she had checked the placenta to make sure it was whole. She discovered a large piece missing. That meant part of the placenta was attached inside Anna and we realized that was very dangerous. I felt Anna should go to the hospital to be safe.

But God's ways are not our ways. The midwife had arrived. When we brought her to the other bedroom to show her the placenta she assured us that it was fine and we shouldn't be concerned. I remembered the Lord said the baby would be safe, but what about Anna?

Since the midwife arrived, Ginny and I both felt it was time for us to go back to the farm. But, I was deeply concerned about Anna, so before leaving, I asked Willie if I could pray. I remember feeling helpless about the missing piece of the placenta. So I prayed, "Jesus, thank You for the safe and speedy delivery. Just as You brought forth

Sagasagay, we ask that everything will be perfectly released into Your hands." Anna looked at me with a funny expression, but neither of us spoke another word. We just hugged and kissed each other.

About half an hour after we arrived home, the midwife phoned. She said that Anna felt the need to use the portable commode by her bed. When she sat down, the missing piece of the placenta dropped out. Thank you, Lord, for your faithfulness.

❧❧

The Lord does complete what He begins. He will be with you when He bids you to come. If you feel overwhelmed or inadequate for a task, put your trust in the Lord. With God all things are possible.

Release Everything To The Lord

Ah Lord God!
Behold,
Thou hast made the heavens
and the earth
by Thy great power
and by Thine outstretched arm!
Nothing is too difficult for Thee,
Jeremiah 32:17

MAN IN A COMA

To open their eyes, and to turn them from darkness to light,
and from the power of Satan unto God,
that they may receive forgiveness of sins, and inheritance
among them which are sanctified by faith that is in me.
Acts 26:18

I received a phone call from a young woman I had never met. She had heard about me from a mutual friend. She asked me if I would be willing to go to the hospital and pray for her father who was in a coma. She was burdened for his soul.

I was scheduled to speak the following morning in Bemidji, which was very close to the hospital. Since Mom Brogger was driving me to the meeting, Shelly said that if she was willing to take me to the hospital, I should go.

On the way to Bemidji, I mentioned the man in a coma to Mom Brogger. I asked her if she would drive me to the hospital. She was always so kind and this time was no different. She replied, "Sure, my dear, we can go right after the meeting." (Lucille Brogger was the original owner of the farm. She was in her seventies, old enough to be our mother. Out of respect for her, we called her Mom. Over the years she proved herself to be a mother to each one of us. She prayed and cared about us as a true Mother in the Lord.)

As we entered the room of the man in a coma, he was extremely restless. His wife was sitting by the foot of his bed. I sat down next to her and introduced myself. I explained that her daughter had phoned me and asked if I would come and pray for her father.

175

His wife replied that her husband wanted to die and she did not want to go against his wishes. He had suffered for many years and was weary from the pain. I told her I didn't want to bring added grief to her at a time like this. However, I repeated that her daughter had phoned and asked me to come and pray for her father. Would that be all right with her? She then told me that would be fine.

I walked to the side of his bed and knelt down. His back was to me, so I called out to him by his name. He instantly turned his head toward me and answered, "Yes?" I was shocked and Mom Brogger put her hand on her mouth, while his wife gasped aloud.

I answered him very calmly, "The Lord has sent me to ask you if you want to know Him." He replied, "Yes, I want to know Him." I asked if he wanted to pray for Jesus to come into his heart to be his Lord and Savior. He replied instantly, "Yes, I would like to pray."

I then led him in a prayer of salvation. He followed like a little child, not missing a word. When we finished the prayer, he immediately turned over and his back was to me once again.

The man in a coma was no longer restless. Mom Brogger and I held his wife in our arms. She thanked us for our visit as we departed.

The following afternoon, his daughter phoned to say that when she had walked into her father's room, he was sitting up in his bed, eating an ice cream cone. We both laughed and rejoiced together.

The man in a coma lived for about seven more months. He read the Bible with his daughter and his wife each morning and evening. He was no longer weary of life. He was now grateful to the Lord for extending his days on earth. He was truly transformed.

⤙⤚

Do you know someone in a coma? Tell them about Jesus. Perhaps they will even respond to you. Try it and see what happens!

Where There Is Life—There Is Hope

Praise be to the God and Father of our Lord Jesus Christ!
In his great mercy he has given us new birth into a living hope
through the resurrection of Jesus Christ from the dead,
and into an inheritance that can never perish, spoil or fade—kept
in heaven for you, who through faith are shielded
by God's power until the coming of the salvation
that is ready to be revealed in the last time
I Peter 1:3-5

GRANDMA ANNA

That if you confess with your mouth, "Jesus is Lord,"
and believe in your heart that God raised him from the dead,
you will be saved. For it is with your heart
that you believe and are justified,
and it is with your mouth that you confess and are saved.
Romans 10: 9, 10

How special are grandparents? My Grandma Anna and Grandpa Adolph were very special to me. I was born during World War II, while my father was in the service and stationed in Alaska. For the first two years of my life, my mother and I lived with my grandparents. I was colicky for almost a year and Grandpa Adolph spent many nights walking me, holding me and loving me.

When the war ended, my mother and I moved to Seattle, Washington, to be with my father. Memories are hidden deep within the heart and I remember my Grandpa Adolph with deep affection. When we returned from Seattle, the only person I asked for was my Grandpa Adolph. Where was he? Why did he not want to see me? Grandpa Adolph had passed on, and I was too young to understand. I could not be consoled.

My Uncle Marty showed pictures of Grandpa Adolph on his projector. I looked behind the screen trying to find him. All I wanted was my Grandpa Adolph to walk with me, hold me and love me.

My brother, Robert, was born when I was three years old. We both had a special relationship with Grandma Anna. She would take us on long walks to the park and we talked together about everything. Grandma would push us high on the swings and run underneath laughing. It appeared as though she enjoyed herself as much as we did, perhaps even more. We would sit in the sandbox together for hours building castles and tunnels. I can still see her shining smiling face, watching my brother and I enjoy ourselves, covered with sand.

Grandma Anna always accepted me just as I was; even if I was naughty, she still loved me. She was a real comfort in my life; she was not just my Grandma, she was my friend.

Grandma Anna loved to talk with me about Grandpa Adolph. He had graduated from a university in Austria, with honors, earning his degree in chemistry. He had a successful business and was quite wealthy. When my mother was about ten years old, Grandpa Adolph lost all of his money in a questionable fire which had burned his business building to the ground. His fire insurance had expired, and a check for the insurance was made out in a stamped envelope sitting on his desk. But all had been lost. Grandpa Adolph was a broken man with a broken heart, never able to forgive himself for not mailing the check.

All of Grandma Anna's brothers and sisters were millionaires, yet I never remember her complaining about her lot in life. I can still hear her saying, "June darling, isn't God good? He is so good to me. I thank Him every morning for life and breath." Her smile lit up her face and she always brought laughter with her, wherever she went.

My Uncle Marty came to our apartment one day to encourage Grandma Anna to marry his neighbor, Charlie. Charlie was a sickly man and really desired a companion. My Uncle Marty thought it would be good for Grandma to marry him, since he had money to support her and she too would have a companion. They did marry and moved to Florida, but Charlie didn't live too much longer. So Grandma Anna moved back to Brooklyn to live with us again for a short while.

It was wonderful having Grandma with us again. We took our walks together and had our special talks, while Grandma cooked all of our favorite meals. She made the best potato pancakes you have ever tasted and her coffee crumb cake was heavenly. Jewish pastries were her specialty, her *kasha* was delicious and her brisket could not be matched.

Grandma Anna decided to move back to Florida, because she had made friends and felt that our family needed time alone. Several years had passed when I received a letter from Grandma Anna telling me that she had met a man named Sam and that they fell in love. She was about seventy-five and Sam was in his eighties. He loved life as much as she did, and they were going to be married. Grandma said she felt like a teenager again.

When Shelly and I married, Grandma Anna brought Sam to our wedding. They walked down the aisle together and Sam prayed the blessing over the *challah* in Hebrew, before our dinner was served. It was an honor to have them with us.

Sam died about ten years later, and Grandma Anna was lonely but remained in Florida. My parents moved to Florida when they retired and Grandma Anna would visit with them for extended periods of time. Aunt Tillie and Uncle Marty moved to West Palm Beach, Florida, so two of her four children were together with her again.

As close as I had been to Grandma Anna, I had never spoken to her about Jesus. I cannot even explain why, since I am usually outgoing about my faith, freely sharing my love for God with everyone. Nevertheless, when it came to Grandma Anna, I had never said a word and I didn't know if my mother had told her. I must confess that I was very concerned about her soul.

In the late seventies, my mother took ill and I went to Florida to care for her. I had a deep sense in my heart that I was going on a mission, sent by God, to tell Grandma Anna about Jesus. She was almost ninety-four and as spunky as ever, still loving life. She was coming to spend several days with us at my parents' condo. Grandma Anna and I were in the kitchen alone. I was by the sink washing dishes when she asked, "So, June darling, how is life treating you? How is Shelly? How are your children?"

I turned my head and asked, "Grandma, did Mom ever say anything to you about my life?" She replied, "Yes, June darling, she told me that you loved God and you now live for Him. I think that is wonderful. I love God, too."

I leaned my hands on the kitchen table for support and asked, "Grandma, do you know His Name?" She looked me straight in the eye and said, "Yes, June darling, I think I do." I asked her, "What is His Name, Grandma?" She responded cautiously, "Jesus Christ."

I was shaken to the core of my being. It was a good thing I was leaning on the table for support, because my legs never would have held me up. I asked how she knew His Name. Very soberly and calmly she told me that my Grandpa Adolph believed that Jesus was the Healer and our Messiah.

My Grandpa Adolph, the one who held me, loved me and walked with me night after night for almost a year…he knew the Lord! I had always wondered why my heart was so open to Jesus, when my Jewish people are so resistant. I used to ask the Lord who had prayed me into His Kingdom. Now I knew, it was my Grandpa Adolph; he was the one. The one whose treasures in life burned to the ground had his treasures stored up for him in heaven. Oh, to think that one day I will see him again.

I asked Grandma Anna, "You know His Name, but do you want to know Him? Have you ever given your heart to God?" I told her that I believed the Lord had sent me to talk to her, so her heart would be prepared to see Him. She wept and exclaimed, "See Him, June darling! I have known three men in my life, how can I see Him?"

It amazed me! Grandma Anna had perceived the holiness of God, and she instinctively knew that she could not see God without a Savior. At that moment, my mother walked into the kitchen very upset and told me that was enough. I felt to honor my mother by ending the conversation.

The following day, Grandma Anna was sitting next to me in the den. I asked her if she remembered our conversation in the kitchen and immediately she began to cry. She said, "June darling, this is the second time you have made me cry." I explained to her that the Spirit of the living God was touching her heart.

My mother was very disturbed and said, "That's enough, June." But this time was different. I realized I was sent to speak with Grandma Anna. I very calmly and gently told my mother that I needed to continue talking with Grandma and if she wanted to stay and listen, she could. My mother did remain in the den.

With tears running down my cheeks, I asked Grandma Anna if she wanted to know the Lord. With tears streaming down her face, she replied, "Oh yes, June darling, but how?" We held hands when Grandma Anna asked the God of Israel, Jesus, to forgive her for her sins and to wash her clean. She asked *Yeshua*, Jesus, to come into her heart to be her personal Lord and Savior. She accepted Jesus as the Messiah. We held each other close and cried together, while my mother sat on the couch—silent.

I cried when Grandma Anna was to go back to her apartment. I knew she would never read the Bible. She did not know another believer. Was she really saved? I asked the Lord to give me a sign, and I also asked Him to please forgive me for even doubting.

When Grandma Anna was ready to leave, she held me in her arms and proclaimed, "June darling, you can say that your mission has been accomplished, and you will be blessed for this throughout eternity."

Those were the last words Grandma Anna spoke to me this side of heaven. My father told me that not too many months later, he had walked into Grandma Anna's bedroom and found her sitting up with her arms outstretched to heaven saying, "Lord, I am ready. Take me home." And, several days later, Grandma Anna went home to be with the Lord.

⋘⋙

Are you afraid to share your faith with your loved ones? Do you fear rejection? Are there obstacles in your way? Pray for grace and speak. Remember Grandma Anna's words, "Your mission has been

183

accomplished..." I look forward to seeing Grandma Anna in Heaven with all the angels and saints rejoicing around the throne of God.

So Be It Lord Yeshua—Amen

I will strengthen the house of Judah and save the house of Joseph.
I will restore them because I have compassion on them.
They will be as though I had not rejected them,
for I am the LORD their God and I will answer them.
Zechariah 10:6

UNCLE MARTY'S SALVATION

The LORD is my strength and song,
And He has become my salvation;
This is my God, and I will praise Him;
My father's God, and I will extol Him.
Exodus 15:2

It was not many years after Grandma Anna went to be with the Lord, that my Uncle Marty was diagnosed as having an embolism on his brain. He was incoherent, resulting in my Aunt Tillie committing him to a nursing home.

While visiting my parents, the Lord impressed me to speak to Uncle Marty about salvation. In years past, he had vehemently opposed Jesus. I asked my mother if we could visit him and she thought that was a good idea.

We had lunch with my Aunt Tillie who opened up her heart to me. She was very lonely and struggling with guilt about putting my Uncle Marty into a nursing home. They had been married for more than fifty years and her heart was broken.

When we arrived at the home, I was surprised to see my uncle looking as well as he did. I had asked the Lord to make a way for me to speak with him. When my aunt tried to feed him, he became unnerved and verbally abusive. My mother suggested they take a walk together. I asked Uncle Marty how he was adjusting to his affliction. He responded, "You learn to acclimate to whatever comes your way in life." He had been so unreasonable with my aunt, I was surprised at his lucid answer.

I asked him if he prayed. He answered indignantly, "Only children pray." I told him that, to God, we are all children whether we are eight years old or eighty. He responded, "Well said."

I asked if he knew the Name of the Lord. He seemed annoyed and answered abruptly, "Ben." I was aware that I needed to press on, so I asked him if he knew that in Hebrew, *ben* meant son. I also asked if he would like to know the Name of the Lord. He replied, "Yes. What is His Name?" I was surprised when he answered yes. I explained that after the Lord parted the Red Sea, Moses sang:

> *The LORD is my strength and song,*
> *And He has become my salvation;*
> *This is my God, and I will praise Him;*
> *My father's God, and I will extol Him.*

I then asked Uncle Marty, "Did you know that the word salvation in Hebrew is *Yeshua*? And in English, it is Joshua and in Greek, it is Jesus. Moses was singing in Hebrew that the Lord had become his salvation, his *Yeshua*, his Jesus. Do you want to know the Lord?"

He looked at me, as his eyes filled with tears and answered, "Yes, June, I want to know the Lord." I led him in a prayer of salvation and Uncle Marty followed like a little baby. He gave his heart to Yeshua, Jesus, as his Messiah and Lord.

It was worth all the pain and the loneliness he had experienced, because the Holy One revealed His Son to my uncle. And, oh, how the angels in heaven rejoiced! I did too.

When Aunt Tillie returned we wheeled Uncle Marty back to his floor and I hugged and kissed him good-bye for the last time, this side of heaven. He sat in his wheelchair with tears streaming down his cheeks, staring at us as the elevator doors closed.

My aunt gasped, "He's crying! That's impossible with the medication he's taking. He has not cried since I brought him here." I told my aunt about Uncle Marty asking Jesus into his heart. He passed on a short time after my visit.

Aunt Tillie passed on just a few years after my Uncle Marty. I have often wondered if she knew it was her time, since she had everything in perfect order. All her bills were paid; everything was taken care of right down to the last detail.

My cousin phoned to tell me about my Aunt Tillie passing on. I wept. My hope is that Aunt Tillie remembered my visit with Uncle Marty, and that she too gave her heart to Jesus, as her Messiah and Lord before she gave up her last breath.

❧❧

Be encouraged to share your faith with someone who appears to be incoherent. Don't believe what you see. Don't believe what you think. Don't believe what you feel. Believe God! Trust and obey His still small voice and you too could see …

The Salvation Of God

May Thy loving kindnesses also come to me, O LORD,
Thy salvation according to Thy word…
Psalm 119:41

SHE'S THE PRETTIEST GIRL
IN TOWN

Ask and it will be given to you;
seek and you will find;
knock and the door will be opened to you.
Matthew 7:7

Scottie was in the National Honor Society in his senior year of high school. He was editor of the school newspaper and served on the student council. He also played baseball on the high school team that Shelly had coached.

One afternoon, he came home from school very excited and said, "Mom, you are not going to believe this. Ann Nieces asked me to go with her to the senior prom. What do you think about that?"

I am convinced that my response did not come as a great surprise to Scottie. Shelly and I had raised our children to wait for the Lord to reveal their mates to them, which meant no dating and I reminded him of that. He became very flustered, as he waved his arms up in the air and exclaimed, "But, Mom, this could mean her salvation. I could tell her about Jesus. How do you know it is not the Lord's doing? And besides, she's the prettiest girl in town."

I encouraged Scottie to pray and be cautious. Shelly always had the final say in our family. Scott's expectation of going to the prom was now in his father's hands. Shelly cautioned Scott, just as I had. He believed that Scott was old enough to have his own convictions, so he left the decision with him.

Scottie was a responsible young man with a deep love for Jesus. He decided to fast and pray for his decision. About a week into his fast, he took his Bible to the lake at Camp Dominion. As he sat on a rock, he prayed, "Lord, should I go to the prom with Ann? What do You want me to do?" He then read from Matthew16:24 these words: *Then Jesus said to His disciples "If anyone wishes to come after Me, let him deny himself, and take up his cross, and follow Me"* (New American Standard).

As he walked back to the trailer, he thanked the Lord for speaking to him. It amazed him that Jesus had left the decision with him, just as his earthly father had also. As Scott walked through the door, he appeared so calm and peaceful. I knew that he had received his answer from the Lord.

As much as Scottie desired to go to the prom, after reading the Scripture, he realized being a disciple of the Lord was more important to him than anything in this world. Therefore, he chose to deny himself by not going to the prom with the prettiest girl in town!

❦❦

May this episode in Scottie's life encourage you to entrust your children to the Lord. Allow them to choose their way, as you pray for them to obey the leading of the Lord. If you are a teenager, may Scott's experience encourage you to ask the Lord His will for you. Then, obey His still small voice and you will be blessed.

Are You Willing To Deny Yourself
Take Up Your Cross
And Follow The Master

For the Son of Man is going to come
in his Father's glory with his angels,
and then he will reward each person
according to what he has done.
Matthew 16:27

HEART TROUBLE

In the thirty-ninth year of his reign Asa
was afflicted with a disease in his feet.
Though his disease was severe,
even in his illness he did not seek help from the LORD,
but only from the physicians.
Then in his forty-first year of his reign
Asa died and rested with his fathers.
II Chronicles 16:12, 13

In August, 1982, we drove to Dallas, Texas, with Scottie who was going to attend Christ for the Nations, a two-year Bible school.

When we returned to Minnesota, my heart longed for Scottie. I missed him so much and to add to my sorrow, I discovered that his best friend had betrayed him.

One morning, I felt a sharp pain like a knife go through my heart. I wondered if this is how it feels to have a heart attack. I asked the Lord to please clarify what I should do and I opened my Bible to II Chronicles 16:12, 13. I was thirty-nine at the time. I believed after reading those verses, I was not to seek advice from a physician. I asked Shelly if he could support me in that decision and he said that he would. I had the sense that Jesus was asking me to trust Him completely with my life, or in my death.

This was an act of faith on my part because it was obeying the Lord. Just as going to a doctor would be an act of faith, if that was what the Lord was speaking. The issue God was uncovering was not about seeing a physician—it was the cause of my heart condition.

For whether we live,
we live unto the Lord;
and whether we die,
we die unto the Lord:
whether we live therefore,
or die, we are the Lord's.
Romans 14:8

I honestly did not know if the Lord would heal me, or if He was going to take me home. I did have the elders anoint me with oil and pray every time we met together. My heart was filled with fear, and I realized that the Lord desired to deliver me from all my fears.

For the next two years, I had constant pain in my chest, neck, arms, shoulders and back. I thank Shelly for his strength and love for me during those years of affliction. He prayed with me every morning for grace and strength to make it through the day. One morning he prayed, "Lord, we know our days on earth are numbered and we cannot add a cubit to our stature. A doctor can tell us that we have six months to live and you might keep us in the earth for many years. Or a doctor could give us a clean bill of health and we could have a heart attack and die before leaving his office. Life and death are in Your hands, Lord."

That prayer created a deeper faith in my heart to persevere. I experienced the Lord beckoning me into a much deeper place of communion with Him. Eternity seemed to become a deeper reality, like never before. Every moment with Shelly and the children were cherished moments, not knowing how much longer we would be together.

My friend, Pearl, a true intercessor, phoned me one morning. I asked her to please pray for me, and if the Lord spoke anything about my affliction, to please let me know. About a month passed, when Pearl phoned to say that the Lord had spoken: *Mend your fences; healing is on its way.*

I understood the message, because I had deep resentment in my heart toward Scottie's friend and his family. Despite God's graciousness toward me, my resentment had deepened. Although I prayed and chose to forgive, I could feel my heart growing harder and colder. I realized that mending my fences meant repentance—a change of mind and heart.

Vera encouraged me to phone Scottie's friend to ask him to forgive me for hardening my heart toward him. Shelly and Vera prayed for me, as I reluctantly dialed his number. My heart pounded when I heard his voice and I asked him to please forgive me for resenting him and allowing my heart to grow cold. He forgave me. Yet his response was so indifferent, it devastated me.

Vera gave me an illustration of a thorn stuck very deep in the palm of my hand. It would be very painful and after I pulled it out, it would still feel as though it was there, but it was gone.

At that exact moment, I felt a deep release in my heart. Something had reversed in my physical being and I knew it. Mending my fences was confession of my resentment and asking forgiveness brought healing on its way.

However, the pain did remain for another year. I realized from the example of the removal of the thorn, that the resentment had caused deterioration of my health, but it had been removed by my asking forgiveness. However, the pain was still real. But healing was on its way. I was completely healed soon after our move to Phoenix.

Several years later at a church service in Minnesota, Scottie's friend's sister was present as they served communion. I knew I could not partake without asking her forgiveness. I knelt down before her with my piece of bread and, with deep sobs, asked her to please forgive me. We shared the bread and wine together as she granted forgiveness to me. We embraced in the presence of the Lord.

I am eternally grateful for the Lord's gift of forgiveness and healing. His touch is healing both to the natural body and to the spiritual man. My spirit, soul and body were refreshed.

❧❧

Are you suffering in your body? The Lord may be allowing a physical problem to alert you to a spiritual root. Ask Him. Obey what He tells you to do. Humble yourself in the sight of the Lord and He will lift you up. The Lord will meet you. He will touch you with His healing right hand, just as He touched me.

Confession Brings Healing

He heals the brokenhearted and binds up their wounds.
Psalm 147:3

KNOW THE HEART
OF OUR FATHER

And He who sent Me is with Me;
He has not left Me alone,
for I always do the things that are pleasing to Him.
John 8:29

Scott was now in his second year at Bible school, Dean was a senior in high school and Suzi was in the seventh grade. Her classes were taught in the high school building.

One morning at breakfast, Suzi told us that she and her best friend, Nancy, wanted to join the cheerleaders. When she finished speaking, it got so quiet at the table that you could have heard a pin drop. Shelly broke the silence by letting Suzi know that he would never allow her to join the cheerleaders. Their mini-skirts were much too short and it was inappropriate for her as a believer to be a cheerleader. The remainder of our time at breakfast was in silence.

Later on that day, I phoned Shelly at his office and asked if we could talk. I compared Suzi's desire to be a cheerleader to the boys participating in sports. If it was not inappropriate for them, why would it be inappropriate for Suzi?

He told me that he would not allow Suzi to be a cheerleader. I suggested it was better for her to make a wrong choice at thirteen, than it would be when she was older. The consequences could be so much greater. She could also resent us for not allowing her to be a cheerleader. Resentment could be a seed that would bring the fruit of rebellion. Suzi could possibly turn against the Lord and His will for her life, as well as turning against us.

Shelly promised to pray. Several days passed before he sat down to talk with Suzi. He told her that he still felt the same way about her joining cheerleaders. However, he realized how much it meant to her, so he gave her permission to try out. Suzi thanked him for demonstrating his love, by taking her feelings into consideration.

Suzi went to every practice to learn the cheers. She was excited about joining the squad and anticipated the tryouts. Everyone knew Suzi was Dean's sister. He was the co-captain of the football and basketball teams and was very popular in school. And, Nancy's sister, Michelle, was captain of cheerleaders, so Suzi was very confident that she would be chosen.

One afternoon as I was ironing, Suzi returned home from school. She hugged me and told me that she did not go to the tryouts for cheerleaders. I was so surprised by her news because I realized how much Suzi desired to be a cheerleader. After getting my composure, I asked her why she did not go to the try outs.

Suzi looked at me with her big, beautiful, bright brown eyes and said, "Mom, you know that I really wanted to be a cheerleader. I just could not do it because I knew that it would not be pleasing to Dad."

Suzi always had a special relationship with her father. Because of her deep love and respect for him, she set an example for us all to follow. That same example was set by Jesus Himself—to always do those things that please the Father.

※☜☞

As a parent, are you willing to trust your child to hear from God? Are you willing to entrust your child to God for His safekeeping? As a child, is your heart open to receive instruction or wisdom from your parents? May we all desire to always do those things that please our Father.

The Love Of God Never Fails

Love (God's love in us)
does not insist on its own rights
or its own way,
for it is not self-seeking...
I Corinthians 13:5

DEAN'S SENIOR YEAR

Endure hardship with us
like a good soldier of Christ Jesus.
No one serving as a soldier
gets involved in civilian affairs—
he wants to please his commanding officer.
Similarly, if anyone competes as an athlete,
he does not receive the victor's crown
unless he competes according to the rules.
2 Timothy 2:3, 4, 5

It was September 2, 1983, Dean's birthday as well as opening day for Cass Lake High School's football season. Dean was co-captain and quarterback of his team. I was excited about their opening game and asked my friend, Sharon, to come and watch Dean play. I was pleased when she accepted.

At half-time, the football team and the cheerleaders sang happy birthday to Dean. Sharon pointed to Michelle, captain of the cheerleaders, and asked me if she was Dean's girlfriend. I told her that Dean didn't have a girlfriend.

Sharon was surprised at my response. She told me not to be naïve and to look at how Michelle was looking at Dean. Sharon again asked if I was sure she was not his girlfriend. I insisted that Dean did not have a girlfriend and that was all there was to it.

When Dean returned home that afternoon, I asked him if Michelle was his girlfriend. His face flushed as he told me that she was. Dean said that he knew he should not be dating and asked me to please be patient with him and to pray. I assured Dean of my love for him and promised to pray.

I must confess, though, I was heartbroken over his decision to date. The Lord had personally spoken to Dean when he was fourteen years old. He told him not to date, but to wait and trust Him for his mate. Dean was aware of the battle in his flesh and appeared sincere about his spiritual struggle. Nevertheless, I was concerned for him because he knew better than to disobey the Lord. I continued to pray for the Lord to strengthen Dean in his faith, and have mercy on him.

As the year progressed, Dean was voted co-captain of the basketball team. He was an example to his teammates. Dean did not curse or drink and being the co-captain allowed him to be a positive influence for his teammates. The bus driver told the principal that the team's behavior on the bus was exemplary. All the teachers, coaches and the boys on the team had a deep respect for Dean.

However, he was still dating Michelle which continued to be a concern to me. I was aware Dean could suffer the consequence of his disobedience to the Lord.

At the end of the basketball season, Dean became very ill. He lost a lot of weight and his coloring was very poor. He was scheduled to go to Germany on a class excursion. His German teacher had phoned to tell me how worried she was over Dean's health.

Janie, a married woman in our community, was like Dean's second mom. She came to visit him and expressed her concern for his physical condition, in light of his dating Michelle. Dean knew how much Janie loved him, so her visit affected him deeply in a positive way.

Dean had been home from school with a high fever for over a week. On his first day back to school, I told him to come directly home because he needed the rest to gain back his strength for the trip to Germany.

That afternoon, Dean phoned to tell me that he was not on the school bus. I was quite upset with him and told him so. He told me that he was going to Michelle's house to end their relationship. What could I say?

Everyone in Dean's graduating class who had applied to college had received their acceptance letters, except for Dean. I realized it was a spiritual matter, because Dean was a very good student. The Lord was waiting for Dean to repent, so He could bless him.

Dean had ended his relationship with Michelle. The blessing was waiting for him upon his return home from Germany. He had received an acceptance letter from The Kings College in upstate New York with a full-tuition scholarship. His repentance had released the blessing.

❧❧

The Lord is very patient, merciful and slow to anger. Are you preventing the blessing of God in your life by making wrong choices? You can turn to God now and repent. In other words, change your mind to agree with the Lord. Do what is right. His blessings will overtake you. His desire is to bless you. He did it for Dean and He will do it for you, too.

Do You Rule Your Flesh Or Does Your Flesh Rule You

Trust in the Lord with all your heart
and lean not on your own understanding;
in all your ways acknowledge him,
and he will make your paths straight.
Proverbs 3:5, 6

VISIT TO PHOENIX

Speak, LORD, for your servant is listening.
I Samuel 3:9b

In August 1984, Louis and Chira Kaplan, of Jewish Voice Broadcast, headquartered in Phoenix, Arizona, came to visit Ben Israel. They requested that we give our testimony for their television and radio programs. When the taping was completed, we bid our farewells to take Dean to The Kings College, in upstate New York. It was as difficult for me leaving Dean, as it had been with Scott. I felt a deep ache within my heart and I wept.

In November, while visiting my parents in Florida, Shelly phoned to tell me that Louis and Chira Kaplan had written. They invited us to labor with them at Jewish Voice Broadcast. Shelly would pastor the Messianic Congregation and preach on their television and radio programs.

We decided to fast and pray. That evening, my mother asked me to go to a service at a Messianic Congregation the following morning. My Jewish mother, asking me to go to a Messianic Congregation —unheard of! I told her I would love to go.

When we entered the congregation, I saw a dear friend, Shmuel, from Israel. I tapped his shoulder and he jumped to his feet and lifted me up in the air whirling me around. He then introduced me to his bride, Pamela. I invited them to lunch at my parent's condo.

At lunch, Shmuel asked about Shelly. I told him about our invitation from the Kaplans. Pamela had lived in Phoenix before she moved to Israel and worked for the Kaplans. Was God preparing me? That evening, I phoned Shelly. He told me about going to a hospital to pray for a man who was on life-support. His wife had requested Shelly to come with Jay, who was a close friend, to pray. In the corridor of the hospital, a woman stopped Jay. She had attended his father's church in Minnesota, when Jay was living in Phoenix. She told Jay that she also wintered in Phoenix. Shelly thought it unusual, on the very first day of our fast, to hear Phoenix mentioned twice in the northern woods of Minnesota. When I told him about Shmuel and Pamela, he believed we should test the waters by going to Phoenix.

He asked Art Beebe for his counsel after reading him the letter of invitation. Art agreed that we should visit Louis and Chira. I made reservations to fly to Phoenix to meet up with Shelly, Scott and Suzi. Dean was still at school in upstate New York. We stayed with Louis and Chira in their home. Shelly preached Friday night at Phoenix Messianic Congregation. Saturday evening, we met with the leaders of the congregation and they all felt we should move to Phoenix and labor with the Kaplans.

Sunday morning, Louis was scheduled to speak at Calvary Church and asked Shelly to preach the message after he spoke about the ministry. Chira asked me to share with her at their Bible study. The Lord gave me a word for Calvary Church at five-o'clock in the morning: *Awake! Awake, O sleeping church!* Many years later, I found a tape by Corrie Ten Boom in the church library. She had spoken that same word to Calvary Church.

During lunch in the fellowship hall, Shelly told me he believed the pastor and his wife should pray with us for wisdom. Amazingly, the pastor then sat down next to Shelly and said he felt he and his wife should pray for us for direction. After lunch, we all went to the sanctuary and knelt together and prayed.

When we arrived back in Minnesota, Art and Mary were waiting up for us. Shelly told them all that had transpired during our visit to Phoenix. Art Beebe told Shelly that if we believed that we were to go to Phoenix, he would bless us and release us.

The following morning, Art Katz walked into our trailer and said, "*Nu,* Shel. So what's this I hear about your going to Phoenix?"

Shelly shared with Arthur and in his unique way, Arthur responded, "My hair is standing up on the back of my neck. I don't want to see you and June go. However, I know it's the Lord calling. I bless your going to Phoenix and I release you. By the way, Pastor Zollner, from Calvary Church of the Valley, is a man of God. He has a burden for our kinsmen, so when you get to Phoenix, you need to contact him." Arthur was shocked when Shelly explained that we had already met Pastor Zollner and we had prayed with him and his wife for direction. The Lord was at work. He had a plan. And, we were experiencing the unfolding of that plan.

ം§.പ

Are you seeking direction? Have you experienced the unfolding plan of God for your life? He will give you all the strength you need to walk out His calling. Trust Him and ask for guidance. The Lord will answer you and bless you in the way you should go.

Called By God

I will instruct you
and teach you
in the way you should go;
I will counsel you
and watch over you.
Psalm 32:8

Shelly, Me, and Art

Part 3

Changes

Seasons come and go
Time has its way of speaking
Calling to the heart of man
Be still and know that I Am God
Changes

Dear Lord help me to be content in You
Help me to see this season through
Your eyes remove the veil
For me to see more clearly
Changes

Deeper pathways made by You
To touch the heart of man
Bring me through this season
Faithful to You
Changes

I cannot see what lies ahead
I only know the One Who called
I trust You Lord through thick and thin
The Faithful One brings
Changes

Summer fall winter spring
In You there's life in each
Teach me Lord to trust You more
The mind of Messiah sees Victory
In Changes

June Volk

OUR MOVE TO PHOENIX

For in him we live and move and have our being.
Acts 17:28a

Packing for our move, and leaving the trailer that the Lord had provided for us for eight-and-a-half years, was accompanied with mixed emotions. Suzi and Rochelle, a single sister serving at Ben Israel at that time, helped pack and organize. Rochelle was moving with us to be Shelly's secretary. We loved her as a daughter and she was a true sister and friend to Scott, Dean and Suzi. Rochelle was a prayer warrior. During the years she labored with us, we experienced victories to further the Kingdom of God through prayer and fasting together.

Waving goodbye to the people in the community, as we drove down the long dirt road, brought tears to my eyes. At the same time, there was an inner anticipation in my heart. We were off on another adventure with the Lord.

The community had loaned us their yellow station wagon for our journey into the desert, which took three days and nights. Brian Beebe was with Scott in the moving van, while the rest of us rode in the station wagon.

We were excited to reach our destination, Phoenix. Jewish Voice had leased a lovely home for us. The hour was late when we arrived, so we carried our pillows and blankets into the house and collapsed on the floor in our bedrooms for the night.

In the morning, the sun shone brightly and its warmth filtered through into our new home. We started unloading the van and unpacking the cartons. About midday, the doorbell rang. A lovely lady from the congregation came to welcome us. She hugged me and handed me a brand new vacuum.

I was amazed because our vacuum was long gone. I had asked the Lord how we were to live in Phoenix. "What should we do if we run out of money? Will we have enough money to buy food? How will I keep the carpets clean without a vacuum? What about a vehicle? Will Suzi adjust well? Will she make friends in school? Is she ready for this move? What will Scott do in Phoenix?"

Before the day had passed, I had a new vacuum. I realized that the Lord's provision would continue in the same "manna" as it had for the past eight-and-a-half years in Minnesota. The only difference in how we were to live was our physical location.

I thanked her for welcoming us and explained that the vacuum was an answer to my prayer. Throughout the years we served Phoenix Messianic Congregation, she was a blessing to us all. That same day the Kaplans visited. Louis prayed and blessed our home and asked for the presence of the Lord to abide with us.

All our cartons were unpacked and our curtains were hung in the living room. All our furniture fit perfectly and our plants warmed each of the rooms. The den had the furniture from our trailer addition. Our kitchen table and chairs fit perfectly in the dinette area. And, we had hung all of the pictures. We thanked the Lord for His help and for the warmth of our new home which was due to His presence.

A collapsible wooden extension table on wheels and a vehicle had been donated to the ministry for us. Scott asked if he could go and get the car with Chira. The expression on his face when he returned was unforgettable. When we saw the car, I understood why. I laughed so hard my stomach ached.

The donated vehicle was a 1955 faded green American Motors Rebel, which had not been driven in years. The rubber foam stuffing came through the upholstery. The dashboard curled up from the intense heat of desert sun baking on it. When Scott turned the key, the windshield wipers started. Nevertheless, this was our means of transportation and the keys were in our possession.

I never did get to drive the Rebel because I could not see over the curled-up dashboard. Remember, I am only 4'11". We covered the upholstery with sheets, so the foam rubber would not get all over our clothing. Its appearance may have left something to be desired, but at least we had our own personal vehicle to take us wherever we needed to go.

The Rebel kept running until Ben Israel decided to scale down on their automobiles. They gave us one of their station wagons and the day their yellow station wagon arrived in Phoenix, our faded green American Motors Rebel died – never to be driven again.

The people in the congregation were precious. We had many years together reaching the Jewish community and touching the local churches. We met on Friday nights for our Shabbat service and had Bible study on Tuesday evenings in our home. We attended Calvary Church of the Valley Sunday mornings because of our respect for Pastor Zollner. We also met in our home on Sunday afternoons for fellowship, and we shared many meals together on the wooden collapsible table on wheels.

Phoenix Messianic Congregation's worship team was heavenly. We danced and rejoiced in Hebraic worship. Scott played the guitar with Dwayne and Steve. Rochelle played the piano and Suzi played her flute. The congregation grew and many souls came to the knowledge of the Lord. We were family. We loved each other. We cared about each other. We gave as anyone had need.

≺ଚ৵≻

God's provision is the same wherever you live. He desires for you to trust Him as He leads and guides you. Listen for His voice and obey Him, without fear. His kingdom comes when love abounds. May the love of God abound through your life.

Where Love Abounds—His Grace Abounds

In a desert land he found him,
in a barren and howling waste.
He shielded him and cared for him;
he guarded him as the apple of his eye,
like an eagle that sirs up its nest and hovers over its young,
that spreads its wings to catch them
and carries them on its pinions.
The LORD alone led him;
no foreign god was with him.
Deuteronomy 32:10 – 12

TRANSITION

Who can proclaim the mighty acts of the LORD
or fully declare his praise?
Psalm 106:2

Rochelle and Suzi read from the Scriptures each morning and evening. Suzi adjusted well in her new school and became friends with Francine, a precious believer. Scott and Rochelle labored with Jewish Voice Broadcast and their income helped buy food for our family and our many guests. After a year in Phoenix, Scott went to Minneapolis/St. Paul to North Central Bible School. Dean came home for a year and labored with Jewish Voice. He was the drummer at our Friday night Shabbat services.

We still attended Sunday morning service with Pastor Zollner and members of Phoenix Messianic Congregation would also join with us. We continued to meet at our home on Sunday afternoon. One Sunday morning, we missed the service at Calvary Church of the Valley. That afternoon, Carolyn, a dear sister and friend, informed us that Pastor Zollner had resigned. Ten years had passed since he had four way by-pass surgery and his arteries were now blocked again. His physician told him to get rid of all stress in his life, so he immediately resigned as pastor.

Ten elders were commissioned to find a new pastor. One Sunday morning, the head elder asked Shelly if he would consider submitting a résumé as a candidate for the pastorate. Shelly declined his offer. However, he did write a letter to the elders with copies to Louis Kaplan and Dick Zollner. He encouraged the elders not to adopt the world's method of filling a position; but to seek the Lord for their pastor through prayer and fasting.

Nevertheless, they continued to receive résumés, and they selected a pastor from Utah to serve at Calvary Church of the Valley. They were waiting for him to be released from his church. Shelly awoke every morning at 5 a.m. to pray. One morning, he heard the still small voice of the Lord tell him, that if the man from Utah turned down the pastorate at Calvary, he needed to reconsider Norm's offer. He was to phone Norm to tell him that he would reconsider being their pastor, if the man they selected declined.

Shelly asked what I thought. I believed the pastor that the elders selected would never turn down being the pastor of Calvary Church of the Valley. With all assurance, I told Shelly that phoning Norm would be fine. We were scheduled to lead a tour to Israel for Jewish Voice. Before leaving Phoenix, Shelly did phone Norm to give him the message. He thanked Shelly and said he would keep that in mind.

At that time, Shelly was the pastor of Phoenix Messianic Congregation. He hosted Jewish Voice Broadcast and preached on television and radio. I interviewed guests on Jewish Voice Broadcast and had a weekly spot, where I shared life experiences and God's intervention. Shelly and I also had a call-in radio program, Hineni (Here Am I). We were sought after speakers for conferences and retreats. The Lord continued to provide for our needs. Our lives were completely involved in God's kingdom being established through the lives of the people He brought our way. Our children were walking with the Lord and growing in God's love.

ॐ

Has the Lord spoken to you? Follow through with what He has told you to do, and watch what happens.

Hear And Obey

Praise be to the LORD,
the God of Israel,
from everlasting to everlasting.
Let all the people say, "Amen!"
Praise the LORD.
Psalm 106:48

FREE TO GIVE

If one of you says to him,
"Go, I wish you well; keep warm and well fed,"
but does nothing about his physical needs, what good is it?
James 2:16

I remember where I was standing at Camp Dominion when I prayed, "Lord, please don't ever put me in a position when I cannot give." Because Shelly had been financially successful, my thought at that time was having enough financial means by which to give. However, over the years the Lord taught me about being free to give and what that really involved.

One summer Dean worked in Phoenix to earn enough money for his fall semester at college. He earned a $1,000, which was adequate for a semester because of his full tuition scholarship and grants.

Dean asked Shelly for some guidance one Tuesday evening before our Bible study. He said he believed that the Lord told him to give money to a couple in our fellowship. Shelly said that would be fine with him. Dean said, "Dad, I don't think you understand. It's a lot of money." Shelly asked if it was $50. Dean told him a lot more. He asked if it was a $100. Dean replied, "Dad, I believe the Lord told me to give $500."

We were not in a financial position at that time to help Dean, so Shelly was silent for a long while. He then told Dean if he believed the Lord told him to give $500, he should obey.

After the study that evening, Dean took the couple into his bedroom and gave them an envelope with the money. When they opened it, Deanie said that they could hardly believe their eyes.

That evening, before coming to the study, they had prayed and asked the Lord to please meet them in their monthly expenses. They had three young children and were in need of exactly $500. No one at the Bible study knew what had taken place.

Two single brothers remained after everyone left the house. They told Dean they had money in their joint account that they never deposited. They had phoned the bank and they even went to the branch office to try to straighten it out. After checking their records, the bank insisted that the funds belonged to them. This had been going on for months, until the brothers decided to ask the Lord if He had intention for those funds. The Lord told the brothers that the money was for Dean. They gave him a sealed envelope and went home.

When Dean related to us what had happened and opened the envelope, his mouth dropped open. In the envelope was a check made out to him for $1,000. The Lord is always glorified when we are obedient to the leading of His Spirit. The needs of a family were met, the needs of a student were met and I learned what it meant to be free to give.

∽◈∾

We usually think of giving in terms of finances only, however, it goes much deeper. When we give out of our own need, we are set free. Are you in need of love? Love someone. Are you in need of forgiveness? Forgive. Are you in need of finances? Be free to give.

God Gave His All

...Freely you have received, freely give.
Matthew 10:8b

HERE COMES THE BRIDE

In his heart a man plans his course,
but the LORD determines his steps.
Proverbs 16:9

In the fall of 1986, Shelly and I hosted a tour to Israel for Jewish Voice Broadcast. The people joining us lived in different parts of the country, so we all were to meet at JFK Airport in New York City. Shelly and I left several days early to visit family in New Jersey.

When we arrived at the airport in Phoenix, we discovered our flight to New Jersey had been canceled. Shelly arranged for a flight on another airline. The only difference from our original flight was our stopover—Detroit instead of Chicago.

In Detroit, as the passengers boarded, their apparel confounded me. They were clothed as if going to a wedding. The ladies wore bridesmaid's dresses and the men wore tuxedoes with boutonnieres in their lapels.

Shelly was preoccupied with reading and had not noticed. I tapped him on his shoulder, and pointed to two people boarding, dressed like a mother and father of a bride or groom. As Shelly observed them, he said, "Look, June, *here comes the bride!*"

When I looked up, there was the bride walking down the aisle all dressed in white. Her face was veiled with her head downward and her eyes were fixed on her bouquet. The groom followed directly behind. She looked so out of place on the airplane. Why would she allow herself to be such a spectacle? I honestly could not believe my eyes. A bride dressed in her wedding gown, with her bridal party in full attire, on an airplane.

Three of the groomsmen sat down across the aisle. Shelly leaned over to ask them why they were dressed in wedding attire. The groomsmen explained they were from Yugoslavia. Tradition calls for the bride to be prepared for her bridegroom to come. She does not know when he will arrive. He could come day or night. Her wedding gown and her bridal party's attire should be prepared for his arrival.

When the bridegroom appears, he takes his bride along with her bridal party, dressed in their wedding garments, to his hometown. The bridegroom's party accompanies him dressed in their wedding attire. The flowers and bridal bouquet are given to the bride and her attendants. She carries her bouquet with her head down until she takes her vows. She can then look into the face of her bridegroom.

As we listened to the Yugoslavian groomsmen explain their tradition, it reminded us of the ancient Hebrews. The bride was to be prepared, as she waited for the bridegroom to come. And as believers, we are waiting for Messiah to come and take us to be with Him.

That evening, I pondered the events of the day. While washing my face and brushing my teeth, the Lord asked, "Are you willing to put on your bridal gown for Me in this world? Are you willing to appear as misplaced in this world, as the bride was as she walked down the aisle of the airplane? Are you willing to live with an eternal perspective and not for the pleasures of this life? Are you willing to live in the expectancy of My coming?"

I pondered His questions for a long while. On one hand, I felt privileged to be asked. On the other hand, could I endure the reproach? Was I really willing to pay the price? Did I love Jesus enough? Would I make a vow and break it?

I bowed my head and told the Lord that I was willing to be His bride, in this world. I asked for His grace and His strength, so I might remain faithful. I realized that I could not fulfill this promise in my own strength. That night, I asked the Lord to please increase my love for Him. I chose His life and His desires over my own. I asked the Lord to please increase my faith.

I believe that the Lord was preparing my heart for our season in the desert. I'm often reminded of the bride on the airplane. No one understood why she was dressed in her wedding garment.

I realize now the faithfulness of the Lord in asking me to make that vow to Him, so many years ago. He has answered my heart's cry. He has increased my faith and my love for Him. The Lord has sustained me, by His Spirit, to continue to walk with Him as His bride, the Bride of Christ.

❦❦

Are you frustrated or discouraged because things are not going according to your plans? Or planes? Has your schedule been messed up? Are you willing to allow the Lord to adjust everything in your life? The Lord desires you as His bride. He is calling you today. May your devotion to Jesus be complete. Remember the canceled flight and the bride on the plane. May your life demonstrate to this lost and dying world:

THE BRIDE OF CHRIST

He who overcomes will, like them,
be dressed in white.
I will never blot out his name
from the book of life,
but will acknowledge his name
before my Father and his angels.
He who has an ear, let him hear
what the Spirit says to the churches.
Revelation 3:5, 6

FROM ISRAEL TO GERMANY
AND BACK

...Holy, holy, holy is the LORD Almighty;
the whole earth is full of his glory.
Isaiah 6:3b

The tour to Israel we hosted for Jewish Voice Broadcast was unforgettable. Marty Goetz, pianist, singer and song writer, along with his wife, Jennifer, both Messianic Jews, were with us. We became family. My friend, Carolyn, joined with us also. We remained in Israel for several weeks after the tour and went on to Germany together.

During the tour we visited a city not usually open to tourists. However, we were privileged to visit the tomb of Abraham and Sarah in Hebron. *Hasidic* men were dancing and rejoicing by the tomb. As I gazed upon the *Hasidic* men worshipping with joy unspeakable, I wept uncontrollably.

While walking in Hebron, I asked the Lord why I had wept. Within the deepest part of my being, joy began welling up. I then rejoiced. I realized Abraham and Sarah had made it. Through all their trials, heartaches and disappointments in the desert, God had brought them through. The *Hasidic* men danced and rejoiced because they believed in the resurrection. They had hope in their hearts for the coming of Messiah. God had brought Abraham and Sarah through the desert and He would bring us through the desert of Phoenix.

We also visited the West Bank. We walked up the high hill into the bunkers. The tanks were still there along with the smell of war and death. We prayed.

I am sure our tour guide will never be the same having heard Marty worship in the open amphitheater in Jerusalem. Rejoicing in songs of praise on the bus was a touch from heaven as well.

After the tour group departed, the five of us remained in Israel visiting with Jewish believers. One evening in Jerusalem, we worshipped the Lord in Donna Greenberg's apartment as Marty played the piano for hours. It was like an Upper Room experience. The presence of the Lord was so powerful; we could barely stand on our feet. I believe the Lord renewed and refreshed us all.

Our time in Germany was equally blessed. We visited The Evangelical Sisters of Mary and had a private visit with Mother Basilea. I wept as Shelly spoke with her. She held my cheeks and kissed me as she departed. Remember Brother Michael? We visited with him and his wife, Margit. He had a wonderful fellowship in Freilassing. Time and distance can never separate hearts that are joined together in the Lord.

We also visited the Brotherhood of Jesus in Gnadenthal. One of the leading brothers was a Jewish believer and dear friend. He was dying of cancer. Our time with him was memorable. He took us to where he was to be buried and we prayed. Returning to the building where the brothers resided, Brother Moses sat in his wheelchair as we stood before the entrance – high majestic wooden doors.

Brother Moses declared we all were about to enter a door that only God could open. I realized that he was being called to follow Jesus in death and we were being called to die for Jesus in life. As Brother Isaac and Shelly carried him up the long flight of stairs to his room, we waved to each other as he went higher and higher until out of sight.

American friends, Tim and Chucky, arranged a meeting on the American army base. Marty sang and Shelly preached a special message on "One Thing". There was a penetration into the hearts of many men and women that day.

That evening, Shelly phoned Suzi and Rochelle to see how everything was in Phoenix. Pastor Zollner had left a message for Shelly. The man from Utah would not be coming to Calvary.

The elders had waited for his release, but it never came. They prayed for the Lord to have him released by a certain date if he was to be their pastor. That date passed. Early the following morning, the man phoned Norm to tell him he had been released. But, it was too late.

We returned to Phoenix and as we opened our front door, the telephone was ringing. It was Norm reminding Shelly what he had promised. Shelly was to meet with him the following morning. Shelly told Norm he would know it was the will of God for him to be their pastor, if Louis Kaplan and the men he labored with at Phoenix Messianic Congregation blessed him and released him. And that is exactly what happened.

On January 4, 1987, Shelly was "prayed in" as the pastor of Calvary Church of the Valley by Dick Zollner and Louis Kaplan. The ten men appointed to find the pastor for Calvary Church of the Valley also prayed for Shelly. But, it was God who sent His man.

❧❧

Are you willing to say *Hineni* to the Lord? *Hineni* is a Hebrew word which means, Here Am I. Take my life—it is Yours.

Sent By God

O the depth of the riches
both of the wisdom and knowledge of God!
how unsearchable are his judgments,
and his ways past finding out!
For who hath known the mind of the Lord?
or who hath been his counselor?
Or who hath first given to him,
and it shall be recompensed unto him again?
For of him, and through him,
and to him, are all things:
to whom be glory for ever.
Amen.
Romans 11:33 - 36

THE LORD'S PROVISION
IN THE DESERT

And my God will meet all your needs
according to his glorious riches in Christ Jesus.
Philippians 4:19

One Christmas, we had so many guests we could have had a sign reading, *Standing Room Only!* I asked the Lord how was I to feed everyone. Where would I get enough food?

A few hours later our doorbell rang. It was Sister Deborah from the Evangelical Sisterhood of Mary, Canaan in the Desert. She held my hands and told me she had brought boxes of food to feed my dear guests. She then reached into her dress pocket and took out ten crisp twenty-dollar bills and put them into my hands. I could not believe it. I called out to God for help and He sent Sister Deborah.

One evening, Sister Rebecca phoned insisting we come to Canaan in the Desert. When we arrived, Sister Margaret showed us her gold station wagon. Sister Rebecca told us it was their gift to us. They had no idea that a young lady living with us had prayed for an extra vehicle, so Shelly would not have to drive her to work. The Lord moved on our behalf again and inspired the Sisters to give us their station wagon.

When Shelly started to pastor at Calvary Church of the Valley, Jewish Voice Broadcast was paying him $8,000 a year for his labors. Calvary Church of the Valley also paid Shelly $8,000 a year for serving as their senior pastor.

At that time, Scott and Dean were in college. Suzi was in high school and we had several young women living with us. We also had a four-year-old girl, named Charisse, who we were raising for her mother. Everyone thought we were financially secure, so they stopped bringing food to the house and all anonymous money gifts ceased as well.

Through Pell grants and scholarships, Dean was able to attend Wheaton College. We were responsible for $8,000 a year for his tuition. We found ourselves in worse shape financially serving two congregations, than we had been serving one. I asked the Lord why He had allowed us to be in such a tight place. He reminded me that He alone was our provider. We were not to rely on a congregation, a ministry or an individual; we were to look to the Lord for everything. How could I have forgotten?

Before we moved onto the church property, Norm told Shelly that Calvary Church of the Valley wanted to buy us a new vehicle. And, we were able to give the gold station wagon to a family in need of transportation.

When we moved into the house on the church property in 1988, the board of elders raised Shelly's salary to $20,000. Louis Kaplan reviewed his salary from Jewish Voice Broadcast and wondered how we had survived on such a low income. He, too, raised Shelly's salary to $10,000 a year. I must confess, I wondered what we would do with so much money.

Only the Lord knew that Scott would be getting married in Ohio. He also knew we needed provision for airline tickets and wedding attire. He was aware that we were to pay for the rehearsal dinner. He knew we would want to buy the breakfast that followed the morning after the wedding for our out-of-town guests. And, the cost of our hotel was no surprise to the Lord either.

Within a year, Suzi married Bill. We now had provision for the wedding that was held on January 14, 1989, on the beautiful grounds of Calvary Church of the Valley, with weather ordered by the Lord. Suzi's wedding was fit for a princess, with a horse-drawn carriage to take her with Bill to their hotel.

Calvary Church of the Valley grew from about eighty members to over five-hundred. The Lord joined hearts and lives together for

His glory and we experienced revival, as well as being family. Many souls were coming into God's Kingdom and learning to live for the Lord and His purposes.

Scottie and Beth labored with us as youth pastors. The youth increased so quickly that Scott asked us to find a children's pastor and he would oversee the teens. Marriages were restored, many barren women conceived, young people got saved and delivered from strongholds. We held annual Israel Conferences which affected the local Jewish community. Missionaries were sent to foreign fields as well. After many years of prayer, the Lord opened the door for prison ministry. We had teams of men and women visiting prisoners and then helping them after their release. Families visited and served at orphanages in Mexico and helped support the children.

Through the years at Calvary, many of our Jewish kinsmen came to the saving knowledge of the Lord. One young man came from a Hasidic background. He lived in Tucson and came to our service at Phoenix Messianic Congregation on Friday evenings. One Sunday, he came to the service at Calvary Church of the Valley. Shelly was serving communion with the elders as Simon walked forward. Shelly looked up at him and said, "What are you doing here, Simon? You can't partake of communion." Simon responded, "I want my Mashiach (Messiah) and I want Him now." All eyes were on Simon, as he accepted Yeshua as His Messiah. He then had the bread and wine as our congregation rejoiced with the angels in heaven.

We had a discipleship school for a year. The students had an intensive time of studying the Scriptures, worship and evangelism. That is how Dean met Trudy; she was one of the students. They married about a year later.

Each of our children along with our grandchildren worshipped at Calvary. Scottie led one of the worship teams and played guitar. Dean played the drums. Suzi sang, signed and played her flute. Those were very precious years.

Our grandchildren came into the world and we treasured our time together with them. When each one was an infant, I was blessed to be able to worship the Lord with them in my arms. Their little hands would be raised up in praise with mine. I believe that something was imparted into their little hearts that will last forever. We were also blessed with many spiritual children and grandchildren.

The church worked through many trials, and we saw the life of God transforming the lives of the people. Then, after almost ten years of serving as pastor, Shelly's leaders turned against him. The people who did not follow them were excommunicated from the church. God's love and acceptance of us, when we experienced rejection and slander from men, broke our hearts.

We thank the Lord for calling us to the backside of the desert, although those years had been difficult ones. He proved Himself as the faithful One to us. Through it all, Jesus revealed Himself as our Counselor, our Healer, our Master and our friend.

ᦒᦒ

While God changes not, our circumstances might. God is calling us to be faithful in the depth of the valley, just as we would be in our mountain top experiences. If you are willing to lose your life, you will find it. Embrace your Cross, so that your circumstances will not overtake you. In your desert experience, the Lord is waiting to meet you.

Don't Be Afraid To Follow Jesus
He Will Be With You Always

Therefore, behold, I will allure her,
Bring her into the wilderness,
And speak kindly to her.
Then I will give her her vineyards from there,
And the valley of Achor (suffering)
as a door of hope.
And she will sing there
as in the days of her youth,

As in the day when she came up from the Land of Egypt.
"And it will come about in that day,"
declares the LORD,
"That you will call Me Ishi (my husband)
And will no longer call Me Baali." (my task master)
Hosea 2:14 -16
(parentheses added)

A DIVINE GRUMP

... Behold, your king is coming to you;
He is just and endowed with salvation,
Humble, and mounted on a donkey,
Even on a colt, the foal of a donkey.
Zechariah 9:9b

Shelly's father, Sol, immigrated to America from Russia in his late teens. When members of his family in New York said they were financially unable to help him, he felt displaced and alone. He roamed the streets of Brooklyn and fear gripped his heart.

Late one afternoon on her way home from grocery shopping, my Great Aunt Mary, Grandma Anna's older sister, noticed Sol alone and looking despondent. Being a kind, gentle, loving soul, she invited Sol to live with her family. She and Uncle Louie cared for Sol as one of their own children.

They owned a hardware store and gave Sol a job. Aunt Mary opened a savings account and deposited all the money Sol gave her for his room and board. When he was old enough to care for himself, she surprised him with a bankbook. Those funds were used to purchase the equipment he needed to begin a wood flooring refinishing business.

While living with my Aunt Mary, Sol befriended a young man named Nat. Their friendship resulted in Sol marrying Nat's sister, Lily. Nat married Aunt Mary's youngest sister, Flora. Only the Lord knew that one day Aunt Flora and Uncle Nat would introduce me to Shelly, Sol and Lily's second son.

Sol and Lily purchased a home in Brooklyn, where they raised their three sons. Their boys were the center of their lives, as was living a Jewish lifestyle.

Sol and Lily welcomed me into their family as they did Rita, Norman's wife. They were loving parents and were delighted when we gave them grandchildren. We all have cherished memories of our family life together.

After Paul and I came to faith in Jesus and Mom was diagnosed as having a malignant brain tumor, Dad's life was turned upside down. When Mom passed on, Dad became reclusive and decided to live alone in their home in Brooklyn. The years following Mom's death were dry and barren ones. His joy in life left him when he lost his beloved Lily. Dad had grown cold, hard and bitter.

Two of his three sons and their wives believed in Jesus, as did his grandchildren. For a devout Jew, this was unheard of. The need for Dad's redemption became essential about fourteen years after Mom's passing. He had developed intense heart problems in his early eighties, so he signed himself into a nursing home, believing he could be rehabilitated and regain enough strength to return to his home.

In 1988, Shelly and I flew to New York to see Dad. He asked us to drive him home to check his mail. As we opened the front door, a deep emptiness and sadness filled my heart. Everything was the same as when Mom was alive. The furniture, the dishes and even the knick-knacks were still in place. Her treasured silver tray that held the *Shabbat* candlesticks was exactly where she had kept them. The rooms were very musty and unkempt. But outweighing the physical appearance, the atmosphere was filled with meaningful memories of our family times together with Mom.

I tried to freshen up the house, as Shelly and Dad filed through the mail that was piled on the dining room table. The time we shared that day brought us closer together than we had been in years. It seemed as though we had never been apart. Shelly planned to speak with Dad about Jesus during our ride back to the nursing home.

When Shelly started to tell Dad about Jesus, the Lord opened up Dad's understanding. Shelly explained that Jesus, in essence, was one with the Father, just as Sol had been one with Lily. He explained the word echad, meaning the oneness of God in the unity of the Godhead, as in the Shema:

Hear, O Israel: the LORD our God is one LORD
Deuteronomy 6:4

Our people went to their death in concentration camps saying the Shema. They would not deny their God, the God of Israel, although they did not know *HaShem*, The Name. By the grace of God, Dad comprehended the meaning of echad. It was our sovereign Lord that opened Dad's eyes to see, and his ears to hear. And, his heart was prepared to believe the good news.

I wept as Shelly led Dad in prayer. He truly believed and accepted Jesus as his Messiah and the Son of God. What a miracle!

As we walked into the nursing home, Dad and I held hands. He was going to the hospital and we helped him pack. While driving there, he hummed and whistled, a sign of contentment that had been absent in his life since Mom passed on.

Scott flew in the following day, and when we walked into Dad's room he was very grumpy, but a new man in the Messiah. He was now A Divine Grump.

A few months later, Dad went home to be with the Lord. The peace of God surrounded his body at the memorial chapel. It was as though the Lord was assuring us of Dad's salvation.

∽᷾᷾᷾

Sol, an orthodox Jew, who prayed in the synagogue every morning after he retired, never would have considered the possibility of Jesus being the Messiah, or of God having a son. Let your heart take courage. If Sol prayed the prayer of salvation, believing that Jesus and the Father are one, God can bring your loved one to faith

in Him. Never stop praying until your eyes behold your answer.
Remember:

Prayer Can Move the Heart Of God
To Change The Heart Of Man

The Lord is not slow in keeping his promise,
as some understand slowness.
He is patient with you,
not wanting anyone to perish,
but everyone to come to repentance.
II Peter 3:9

STEPPING ON THE LIFE LINE

And I will do whatever you ask in my name,
so that the Son may bring glory to the Father.
John 14: 13

Early one morning, as Shelly was praying in his office, Renny, a man in our congregation phoned. His friend Ron had been hit by a car as he was crossing the street. The impact tossed him up in the air and he landed head first onto the pavement. He was in a coma and in the intensive care unit. Renny wanted us to anoint him with oil and pray for a miracle. Shelly agreed so we, along with Renny and his wife Nancy, drove to the hospital.

The nurse in front of the door to the intensive care unit did not notice us as we walked through. We were amazed. We then passed the nurses' station without anyone even asking us where we were going. We walked into Ron's room and saw that both of his legs were in casts and in traction, tubes were in his nose, his head was fully bandaged, he was on oxygen and was hooked up to many other machines.

Ron had not moved a muscle since he was admitted to the hospital. His nurse asked us not to stay too long, since his monitor had registered increased activity ever since we arrived. We thanked her and promised that we would leave after we prayed.

Shelly anointed Ron's forehead as we all laid hands on him and prayed. Ron started to move different parts of his body, so we were encouraged and prayed even more fervently. He moaned while his movements increased.

As we prayed fervently and thanked the Lord for touching Ron, his nurse came running into the room frantically declaring, "Someone is Stepping On The Life Line!"

Renny, who weighed well over three-hundred pounds, looked down and gasped as he realized he was standing on Ron's oxygen line. When he removed his foot, Ron settled down and was as still as when we first walked into his room.

We were horrified! We had almost killed him! We came to see Ron healed and when he moved, we thought Jesus had touched him. Instead, Ron was fighting for his life.

The four of us broke out into uncontrollable laughter. In the elevator, walking to the car and driving home we could not stop laughing. Even when we returned home, we could not comprehend what had happened. We were menaces! So I thought.

The following morning, Nancy phoned and told me that I was not going to believe what occurred. Ron's father had phoned her from the hospital to tell her that when he walked into Ron's room, Ron spoke to him. He got so frightened, he ran out to the nurses' station to tell her that his son had spoken to him.

The nurse told him that it was impossible for his son to speak. It would be a miracle! His father tried to convince her that Ron talked to him. He told her to go to his room and see for herself. Sure enough, Ron was out of his coma, fully alert and talking.

∽჻෫

Do you think that Renny's Stepping On The Life Line had shocked Ron into being healed? *Oh ye of little faith!* Remember Stepping On The Life Line and be courageous. Never fear to serve the Lord with what He asks. If you should feel inadequate for the task – remember, if Jesus could use Renny, Nancy, Shelly and me to pray for Ron's healing, He can equip you and bring about His plan through you – if you make yourself available.

Nothing Is Impossible With God

But God chose the foolish things of the world
to shame the wise;
God chose the weak things of the world
to shame the strong.
I Corinthians 1:27

CELIA'S DREAM

As for me, I will call upon God;
and the LORD shall save me.
Psalm 55:16

Steve was our dear friend, as well as the caretaker at Calvary
Church of the Valley. He was an evangelist and his wife, Celia,
was a missionary from Mexico. They lived on the property and had
been laboring with us for about four years.

Prior to our knowledge of any problems we were about to face,
the Lord warned all of us through a dream that He gave to Celia.

She phoned me one morning quite upset. Celia said that she
had a dream she wanted to share: Satan had appeared in her dream.
He pointed out a small group of people praying. Shelly and I were
among them. Satan said, "See those people, Celia? I hate them and
I want to kill them, but I can't because they are praying." After he
spoke those words, he departed.

Satan appeared a second time to her in the dream and said,
"Celia, I hate you and I want to kill you, but I can't because you
are praying." Celia was really scared and asked if we could pray
together.

Neither of us had any idea as to what extent Satan was about to
pursue our lives, our marriages, our families and our callings. Yet,
in the years that followed, his attack became reality. However, the
Lord had proved Himself faithful to us by preparing our hearts for
battle and had strengthened our faith to endure.

God allowed the dream for our good. Satan desired to scare Celia and to paralyze her faith. But he cannot prevail! He revealed his plan to kill her and gave her the solution for her to prevail—prayer.

As I write, this dream continues to be fulfilled. We have not yet seen the victory in the natural realm, but Shelly and I, along with Celia, are still praying. We know that the Lord is faithful and Celia's dream allows us to know that through prayer the Lord will prevail. Jesus is Victor!

∽⭗⭗

Never fear, keep praying. Let Celia's dream encourage you and cause you to remember …

Satan Cannot Kill You—If You Keep Praying

You are not alone if you are facing fiery trials. The Lord warned us that in the world we would have tribulation, but to be of good cheer, He has overcome the world. Let your heart take courage. Satan might plan an attack, but you can foil his plan through your prayers.

Remember When Trouble Comes Your Way

KEEP PRAYING

… The effectual fervent prayer of a righteous man
availeth much.
James 5:16b

Despair

When you feel you are in despair
Know I am there
Despair—No
Be sure not to fear
I am here—Is that clear
Jesus your bridegroom is near

You are never alone
When you are in the flesh
Fear is known
Calm your soul
Know in the Spirit you are whole
My life is in you

My hand is not too short to comfort too
I died and rose again for you
Cry aloud—Draw near to Me
While in despair
I desire to give to you
VICTORY

June Volk

BETRAYED AND REJECTED

He was despised and rejected by men,
a man of sorrows, and familiar with suffering.
Like one from whom men hide their faces
he was despised, and we esteemed him not.
Isaiah 53:3

If you have experienced loneliness, rejection or even betrayal, you are not alone. Have you ever thought of how painful it was for Jesus to come to His own and His own reject Him? The Lord has walked before you and He is with you. He will help you in ways that will increase your faith to persevere and continue to walk on.

If ye be reproached for the name of Christ,
happy are ye; for the Spirit of glory and of God
resteth upon you:
I Peter 4:14a

I remember many a night weeping and telling the Lord how lonely I was, but letting Him know that I would rather be lonely with Him than without Him.

When I was first saved, I experienced the Lord's intervention when I would have despaired. One morning, about a year before Shelly believed in Jesus, I was feeling extremely lonely. We had lost an intimacy in our marriage because of Jesus, and it deeply grieved my heart. My family and friends had distanced themselves from me because of my faith in Jesus and I was in despair. I wept and told the

Lord how lonely I was, but again, I would rather be lonely with Him than without Him.

While crying and pacing my living room floor for quite awhile, I heard my door bell ringing. I did not want to answer it because my eyes were swollen from crying. I was embarrassed.

The person ringing the bell was persistent, so reluctantly I opened the door. Standing patiently before me was a delivery boy from a florist shop, holding a large rectangular box. I had been crying for such a long time that my thoughts were scattered. It was not my birthday, it was not our anniversary, Shelly and I did not have a fight. Who would be sending me flowers and why? I thought surely he must have the wrong house and I told him so. He asked if I was Mrs. Volk. The flowers were for me.

As I opened the box, I gazed upon the most beautiful long stemmed red roses with a note from Shelly that read, "Hang in there, Junsey." Over the years, when I have suffered for the Name of Jesus, roses have been given to me as a sign from the *Rose of Sharon* that I am loved and accepted in the beloved.

I had suffered from slander against my character for many years and it had taken its toll on my life. I had received hurtful letters from people I had loved and served with all of my heart, and the pain of betrayal and rejection had been overwhelming.

One afternoon, Shelly got the mail and there was a letter I had written in response to a hurtful one I had previously received. My letter had been returned, unopened. I had asked forgiveness for any hurt that I had caused and wrote of my deep love and appreciation for the person involved. It was never read.

I sat by our dining room table looking out the window for a long while. I was deeply grieved. I cried and asked the Lord how that person could not have known how much I loved him. The Lord responded, "June, how many people know how much I love them? How many people even care that I exist? I created every man, woman and child that ever walked the face of the earth. I desire for them all to be with Me throughout eternity. How many people in the world today really know Me?"

I then wept for the Lord. I understood in a very small way His heartache and pain for His children. I also prayed and cried for the person who had returned the letter, unopened. Touch his heart, Lord.

For it has been granted to you on behalf of Christ
not only to believe on him, but also to suffer for him...
Philippians 1:29

During a meeting with pastors and wives, a question was presented that each one was to answer. "What is success to you?" I was unsure of how to respond.

After hearing some responses, I thought deeply about what I should say when it was my turn. What was success to me? The time had come; I was next to give my thought on success. "Success for me," I said, "would be for all my children and grandchildren to follow the Lord and to love Him with all their heart, soul, mind and strength." My answer shocked most of the people present; I confess it surprised me also.

The Hebrew word for success is *saw-kal'*, spelled phonetically. It means to be prudent, to turn the mind to, to be understanding, to be successful and to act wisely, etc. At the time of my response, I was unaware of the deeper meaning of the Hebrew word for success. I now realize that the Lord Himself guided me in my reply.

I did not think much more about it until it was brought to my attention that the pastor, who had asked the question, spoke of my response at his Sunday morning service. It was then that I realized that success in the church today is measured, for the most part, in the same manner as the world would regard success. That entails a pleasing of one's self, rather than a self denial to please God. And, perhaps unintentionally, but nevertheless so, when we touch the heart of the matter, it is a form of betrayal of God.

The avoidance of the Cross and seeking success that the world applauds might keep us safer and perhaps even escape the experience of betrayal or rejection. However, it is deceptive; it only feels safer. In reality, it is a ploy of the enemy to keep us from divine success.

The truth is, the embracing of the Cross sets us free to love and forgive and do exploits for God and for His Kingdom. The character of the Life of Jesus that is produced within a soul who has experienced betrayal or rejection, and has received the faith and grace to persevere and continues to love, is not accomplished in a moment of time.

The Master Potter works tenderly, as the wheel turns and reshapes the clay. As we put our trust in the Hands of the Lord, He accomplishes His transforming work within us. He is the Master indeed.

To be able to love through betrayal or rejection is of God. The victory is accomplished in our hearts because Jesus is alive. The pain and rejection He suffered and overcame on the Cross will enable you to have the victory as you choose to deny yourself, take up the Cross and follow Him.

Because we are so drawn downward by the pulls of this world and this present age, eternity seems like something in the future rather than something we can enter into now. When we accept Jesus as our personal Lord and Savior, we enter into eternity. We should then be living for Him alone and for His eternal rewards. Eternity is a quality of life not just measured in quantity of years.

> *"The world is not a playground; it is a schoolroom.*
> *Life is not a holiday, but an education.*
> *And the one eternal lesson for us all is*
> *how better we can love."*
> Henry Drummond (1851-1897)

❦

Have you loved with all that is within you and are now experiencing rejection? Have you been betrayed? You are in good company. Turn to the Lord who *was despised and rejected by men,*

248

a man of sorrows, and acquainted with grief. He will bring healing to your broken spirit and your broken heart. Take courage. He can restore your hope and joy in Him. Because He did it for me, I know that the Lord can give to you ...

The Victory—To Overcome

The sacrifices of God
are a broken spirit;
a broken and contrite heart,
O God, you will not despise.
Psalm 51:17

He who is victorious
shall inherit all these things,
and I will be God to him
and he shall be My son.
Revelation 21:7

Less of Me, Lord, More of You

Help me Lord to live by Your Spirit
Help me Lord to live my life in You
Not what I feel or think
But to reflect You in the things I say or do
Less of me Lord more of You

You are so patient with me
Long-suffering is who You are
I am quick to answer quick to react
Bring me to repentance that my life might be hid in You
Less of me Lord more of You

In life's conflicts help me to see the other's view point
That I might have the heart to agree
To see healing come
Help me take the offenses and not be
too quick to speak or act
Less of me Lord more of You

I know that what I'm asking will be impossible
for me to handle
So I trust You to meet me in my moment of need
I thank You Lord that when my life ends Yours begins
Because You are faithful and true You never fail
I can say less of me Lord more of You

You turned the other cheek
You suffered the rejection
You said forgive them Father
They know not what they do
Less of me Lord more of You

Forgive me Lord for misrepresenting Your love
You are patient kind gentle forever caring
You died that I might have life
Help me Lord to live for others
Less of me Lord more of You

Cause Your life to grow in me
Cause my life to glorify You
Cause me to be faithful to You Lord
Cause my heart's cry to be realized
Less of me Lord more of You

June Volk

THE LORD'S PRESSURE COOKER

*Then those who feared the LORD talked with each other,
and the LORD listened and heard.
A scroll of remembrance was written
in his presence concerning those who feared the LORD
and honored his name.*
Malachi 3:16

For the past twelve years, the testing of my faith has greatly intensified. Through it all, the Lord's graciousness to me has deeply touched my heart. He has met my every need touching my body, soul and spirit. The evidence of His presence being with us and His love for our family has been undeniable.

I have compared these years to Joseph and Job experiences. I have compared myself to Joseph because it was my brothers and sisters who betrayed me and had me thrown into a pit. I can relate to Job because I said, as did Job: *The LORD gave and the LORD has taken away. Blessed be the name of the LORD.* Job 1:21b (New American Standard)

The week before Shelly was installed as pastor of Calvary, I had attended a meeting for women. The topic was love and how it never fails. During the years Shelly served as pastor, I realized that I failed in truly loving the people. I discovered that unconditional love was not in me, apart from the love of God. My love came to an end, but God's love is eternal.

*Love endures long and is patient and kind;
love never is envious nor boils over with jealousy;*

is not boastful or vainglorious, does not display itself haughtily.
It is not conceited—arrogant and inflated with pride;
it is not rude (unmannerly), and does not act unbecomingly.
Love (God's love in us) does not insist on its own rights
or its own way, for it is not self-seeking;
it is not touchy or fretful or resentful;
it takes no account of the evil done to it—
pays no attention to a suffered wrong.
It does not rejoice at injustice and unrighteousness,
but rejoices when right and truth prevail.
Love bears up under anything and everything that comes,
is ever ready to believe the best of every person,
its hopes are fadeless under all circumstances
and it endures everything (without weakening).
Love never fails...
I Corinthians 13:4 - 8

Shelly's heart, as well as mine, was to see the church mature in the ways of the Lord. He was a faithful servant in loving the people. Unlike me, Shelly thought the best and hoped the best for everyone, even when his leaders turned against him. He readily acknowledged his weak areas and looked to his leaders for assistance. He was unaware that they were about to bring a sordid indictment against his character. It broke his heart as it did mine.

As a result of his leaders' actions we, along with everyone who did not agree with them, were excommunicated from the church. Since our home, as well as the homes of many who labored with us, was on the church property, we found ourselves homeless and separated from loved ones.

We had heard about church splits but never could have fathomed the devastation that accompanies one. Shelly believed he was to continue serving the remnant of the congregation as their pastor. We held meetings at a local school until we found a church building to lease. The Lord faithfully provided finances to lease the building, and we were able to assist the families who had lost their homes.

Shelly and I went from house-to-house for the three and half years following the split.

When I first discovered the slander, I found my heart growing hard and cold. I knew the appropriate prayers, and I did pray blessings for the people involved; however, deep within my heart of hearts, I desired for them to suffer the same pain they had caused the entire congregation. All of our children, both natural and spiritual, were affected by the slander.

I knew my perception was not pure, and I realized I needed a change of heart. I cried out to the Lord to touch my heart and to transform me. I was also aware that if the Lord did not soften my heart, I could lose my intimate communion with Him. It was as though Jesus was asking me, as He asked Peter, "Do you love me?" It was then that Jesus' exhortation to Peter took on a deeper meaning for me.

Tend My Lambs. Shepherd My sheep.
John 21:15, 16

I really did not want to go on serving God's people; it was just too painful. "Lord, I have failed You; please forgive me," I prayed.

I understand now that the Lord wanted me to grow up in Him. He desired to give me a mother's heart for His children. It is very painful to be a mother in the Lord, to love in word and deed, unconditionally. That can only come from the Lord and I asked Him to please put His unconditional love into my heart for all of His children.

If we are His servants, I truly believe that nothing can touch us unless God ordains it, or allows it. I realized that God had allowed the slander, the church split and the devastation. However, I also trusted in His Word:

And we know that in all things God works for the good of those who love him, who have been called according to His purpose.
Romans 8:28

I came to the realization that in our darkest hours of suffering, it gives God the greatest opportunity to reveal Himself to us as He really is. We can learn more about His heart as He guides us through all the adverse circumstances.

I have learned that Jesus is a friend who is with you always. I heard His still small voice encouraging me to press on. I am grateful for these years of testing, as I have learned of His sovereignty and of His faithfulness. I am eternally grateful to Jesus for healing my heart by removing a root of bitterness that manifested during the church split.

Since we are a fast-food generation, we want to see results and be satisfied immediately. However, the Lord is looking for us to be transformed into His image and likeness through the trials and tribulations of life. His desire is to bring us peace within while we are in this fallen world. What appear to be adverse circumstances can be a blessing, if we find the Lord in them. I have learned to ask Jesus in and through all things, "What are you trying to teach me?" By not focusing on the people involved in the conflict, I have discovered that it has kept my heart at peace and close to the Lord.

Life's conflicts, along with God's intervention, can be compared to cooking with a pressure cooker. Since our insides can come to a boiling point, it is important for us to know how cooking with a pressure cooker operates.

What the pressure cooker actually does is increase the temperature by using pressure and steam to raise the temperature higher than the boiling point in order to kill all harmful bacteria. This can be compared to the toxins that are released in our bodies from our volatile reactions during stressful situations. The Lord desires to intervene and heal us from our reactions as we learn to trust Him in a deeper way.

The hurts we experience can develop into anger or hatred. If not tended to, hatred can lead to revengeful murder. We may attempt to cover up our pain with drugs or alcohol, and our hearts can get so hardened that our conscience becomes seared, no longer able to recognize the difference between right and wrong, between good and evil.

As the pressure cooker is used for preserving foods, it also purifies them. Therefore, our pressure cooker experiences can purify us as well as preserve us, if we allow the Lord to work in us through them. Take courage and turn to the Lord for help.

Pressure cookers work at different pressures and for different time periods for different products. Some people might appear to have easier lives than others. Only the Lord knows what it will take for us to respond to His bidding. That is why Paul exhorts us in his letter to the Corinthians,

Not to compare ourselves amongst ourselves...
2 Corinthians 10:12

If we have grown tough, due to our reactions through our circumstances, the Lord might allow challenging pressures to come our way in order to tenderize us. The pressure cooker process tenderizes as well as purifies. What an encouragement to know that the pressures of life can be used by God to soften our hearts, as we allow Him to accomplish His work in us.

There is also a cooling off period to complete the pressure-cooking process. The jars need to cool down, undisturbed. You cannot put them under cold water when they are too hot, because they will crack, destroying the contents. Also, in our life experiences, we too might need time to cool off within, undisturbed.

As a result, the Lord might allow our circumstances to be filled with pressures, turning up the heat, in order to reveal Himself and change us from our mistaken ways or harmful reactions. His pure life transforms our life during increased difficulties by His going through the pressures of life with us.

So, let your heart take courage if you are going through a Joseph or Job experience, or if the Lord is disciplining you, or if you are going through the process of being proved like Abraham. The Lord knows how high to allow the heat to be turned up, how long to allow it to continue and even how long to allow it to cool down.

સ્જાજી

The Lord's Pressure Cooker is a process that both purifies and preserves your life. Exercise patience and do not attempt to short circuit His pressure cooker process. And, you will come through preserved, purified and tenderized...

In The Hands of The Master

For I know that my Redeemer lives,
and that in the end He will stand upon the earth.
And after my skin has been destroyed,
yet in my flesh I will see God...
Job 19:25, 26

Lessons to Learn

Are you learning your lessons well
Do you have a story to tell
Do you believe in hell
Or do you feel in your heart
To rebel
Rebel against what

Don't rebel against God's Word
Believe in Jesus the Messiah
Have you not heard
Obey what God's Word tells you to do
Then you will discern
What is right and true for you to do to learn

What you gain might be pain
But it is worth it all
When God calls you friend
Jesus learned obedience
By the things He suffered
Will it not be true for us too

Lessons to learn
Lessons to learn
What will I gain but pain
To love at all times is gain
How can I learn

Jesus is our example
He walked in the Spirit
He lived to please His Father
He loved till the end
He forgave at every bend
His life is alive within us

But He was the Son of God
For me to love at all times is odd
I don't feel it would be true
Do you
What if I don't feel love
What do I do

Lessons to learn
Lessons to learn
What do I gain but pain
To love at all times is gain
How can I learn

Love is not a feeling it is a choice
As is forgiveness
Can you hear His voice
Forgive them Father they know not what they do
For us also this is true
For whatsoever they do to you they do to Him too

Hatred spite jealousy envy
To name a few
Are not in His life
His life is pure
When we walk in His Spirit we can love
Because God is love

Lessons to learn
Lessons to learn
What will I gain but pain
To love at all times is gain
How can I learn

Let your heart take courage
The Lord delivered me through pain
His Life fills our vessel to overflowing
His Love is the answer for All
Who cry out to Him
On the Name Jesus—Call

He will teach you as He taught me
His mercies never come to an end
He will hold you in His Everlasting Arms
And deliver you through your pain
His Eternal Love
His Life you will gain

Peace be with you Shalom
May His Grace abound
The True answer to life's pain
Yeshua Our Risen Lord
Call on His Name
Lesson Learned

June Volk

Alysa and Me

OUR DWELLING PLACE

... Foxes have holes and birds of the air have nests,
but the Son of Man has no place to lay his head.
Matthew 8:20

The Scripture above was brought to mind over and over again. I took it to heart and trusted that, in due season, the reason why I was unable to stop thinking about it would be revealed to me. I just never expected the lesson to be so prolific.

Holes for foxes are their habitat just as nests are for birds, their own dwelling, and a region where they naturally grow or live. It is as unnatural for birds to dwell in holes as it is for foxes to dwell in nests. Likewise, for man to be homeless is unnatural. Being homeless is very unsettling; however, spiritually speaking, it presents an entirely different picture.

When we lost our home through the split, we found ourselves thrust into a deeper place of dependence upon God. We believed we were not to rent an apartment or lease a house. The dwellings provided for us were sometimes for months, sometimes weeks and sometimes even for days. Ever since the Lord had called us to trust Him and live by faith, He always provided a place for us to live.

We were not sure what the Lord was going to do with the congregation, and it seemed like everything was in a holding pattern. We knew we were to continue meeting unless the Lord indicated otherwise. The church building we leased was in a complex that was sold, and the new owners wanted to convert the building into offices. We leased the building on a month-to-month basis, so naturally and spiritually, nothing was permanent to say the least.

Biblically speaking, we should all live with that attitude, since everything of this world is temporal. When that becomes reality through experience, it is obviously very upsetting to the natural man. Yet spiritually we learn as Paul:... *for I have learned to be content whatever the circumstance*, from Philippians 4:11b.

The Lord gave me a vision while speaking with a woman in distress:

I saw two fields. One was beautiful, filled with green plush grass as far as the eye could see. There was a large weeping willow tree that grew beside a pond filled with swans gracefully swimming. Under the weeping willow was a swing set, waiting for children to come and swing with their hair blowing in the soft breeze. Beyond the pond was a beautiful European style home. The grass appeared so inviting that I desired to run on it barefooted. The scene was tranquil and gave the impression that one could rest from the heat of the day and be protected. However, as the Lord raised me up above the field, I saw land mines, hidden traps, that could explode and kill those walking on that field.

The second field was barren. The land was parched from the heat of the sun. It was not the kind of field anyone would desire to walk through. It appeared as though it would be hard on a person's feet. There weren't any trees to shield one from the heat of the sun and the ground was very stony. However, as the Lord raised me up above the field, I saw hidden treasures: diamonds, rubies, emeralds, and sapphires, etc. There were enough treasures hidden on that field to keep one secure during this life, but the only way to discover the treasures was to walk through that field.

I shared the vision with the woman and I encouraged her to find the will of the Lord for her life and there, she would find the hidden treasures. The Lord's will could appear to be barren and difficult, yet the joy found in those hidden treasures of His life would be inestimable.

When the Lord enlightened the following Scriptures to me, I realized the opportunity He had given us to discover the truth of His Word through our experiences.

LORD, YOU have been our dwelling place
Throughout all generations.
Psalm 90: 1

HE WHO dwells in the shelter of the Most High
will rest in the shadow of the Almighty.
I will say of the LORD,
"He is my refuge and my fortress,
my God, in whom I trust."
Psalm 91:1, 2

If you make the Most High your dwelling—
even the LORD, who is my refuge—
then no harm will befall you,
no disaster will come near your tent.
Psalm 91:9, 10

⸎

If you are going through what appears to be devastation in your life, remember the hidden treasures to be found in the barren field. Do not be afraid to take a step of faith onto a field that appears barren. The Lord will meet you in a marvelous way and your soul will find rest. He will go before you and make the way for you to discover His …

Hidden Treasures

LORD, you have assigned me my portion and my cup;
you have made my lot secure.

The boundary lines have fallen for me in pleasant places;
surely I have a delightful inheritance.
I will praise the LORD, who counsels me;
even at night my heart instructs me.

I have set the LORD always before me.
Because he is at my right hand, I will not be shaken.
Therefore my heart is glad and my tongue rejoices;
my body also will rest secure.
Psalm 16:5 - 9

A MOTHER OF ZION

These things I have spoken unto you,
that in me ye might have peace.
In the world ye shall have tribulation:
but be of good cheer;
I have overcome the world.
John 16:33

There are many joys and many sorrows in being a mother after the heart of God. While assisting Mirela through her time of labor with her first child, the Lord enlightened my heart to a deeper meaning of mothering and birthing. Mirela is Romanian and when she was in labor, she spoke very little English. Through the numerous complications she experienced, I learned many spiritual lessons.

And we know that in all things God works for the good of those
who love him, who have been called according to his purpose.
Romans 8:28

When we are in intense pain and going through a difficult situation, we could lose sight of the promises in God's word. Mirela was not familiar with the English language just as we are not familiar with heavenly perspectives. We become insecure, frightened and when we lose our peace during a time of trial, the Lord desires to awaken us to His presence during the test. He also desires to make us strong in faith, as we take courage and find our rest in Him.

Mirela experienced double trouble during her time in labor. Her first complication, not dilating properly, required pitocin to be given to her which would quicken the process of dilation. Her pain grew so intense, they had to give her an epidural which is a local anesthesia that numbs pain. The pitocin was not working properly, so they decided to break her water bag which caused the baby to go into distress. Her doctor then performed a procedure called amnio-infusion which flushes fluid back into the patient, having the effect that the water bag had never been broken. Her labor pain persisted, growing more intense. Mirela's doctor realized the epidural was not working properly, so they re-injected the epidural fluid, hoping it would take effect. Mirela was discouraged, to say the least.

Finally, the pitocin started to work and she began to dilate. However, another complication occurred when the baby did not drop properly into the birth canal. The doctors were perplexed and Mirela grew increasingly distressed and frustrated. She could not understand why the Lord was allowing this to happen.

Her husband, Doru, tried to comfort her as best he could. He told her that sometimes the Lord allows those who are the closest to Him to experience the deepest sufferings. Jesus can entrust suffering to those who know how much they are loved by Him. Doru had learned much about suffering in Romania, as his father had been in prison for his faith during the Communist regime.

After many hours of labor, the doctors decided to deliver the baby by C-Section. Mirela had hoped to give birth naturally. Nevertheless, we all gave thanks to the Lord that we were not in a hospital in Romania, but rather in America where we are equipped to handle such birthing complications. We asked the Lord to guide the doctor's hands during the surgery and for Mirela's heart to be at peace.

As they wheeled Mirela down the long corridor, I somehow felt relieved for her, realizing her time of travail would soon be over. Within an hour, Doru walked into the nursery with Naomi, their new, beautiful, baby daughter.

Doru explained to us that during the surgery they discovered that the umbilical cord was wrapped tightly around Naomi's neck. Had she dropped into the birthing canal, Naomi would have strangled herself. We were all so grateful to the Lord for His faithfulness to Doru, Mirela and Naomi. Mirela realized that the complications that had occurred during her labor really did work together for the good. The Lord's hand had preserved and protected their baby. He spared Naomi's life!

I have discovered that hardships and suffering may lead us in one of two directions. We can either grow hard, cold and cynical or, we can become broken bread and poured out wine. We can choose to cleave even more closely to the Lord for help. He is our hope and the One Who gives us the strength to endure. Help us, Lord, to trust in You more and more every moment of every day.

Thou art my God, and I give thanks to Thee;
Thou art my God, I extol Thee.
Give thanks to the LORD, for He is good;
For His loving kindness is everlasting.
Psalm 118:28, 29

⤨⤸

Are you going through a time of pain, or are you in distress? Are you frustrated because you are unable to alter your circumstances? Remember Mirela and her time of labor. The Lord was with her and spared her baby. He will be with you in your time of distress. Becoming a mother of Zion is painful. Birthing the Lord's life within does bring trauma to our flesh and to our soul. But remember...

After The Birthing Process—There Is Much Joy

Whenever a woman is in travail she has sorrow,
because her hour has come;
but when she gives birth to the child,
she remembers the anguish no more,
for joy that a child has been born into the world.

269

Therefore you too now have sorrow;
but I will see you again,
and your heart will rejoice,
and no one takes your joy away from you.
John 16:21, 22

The Heart of a Mother

Help me to have the heart of a mother
A nurturer one who loves and cares
Like none other
Help me to call out to You Lord
For my children

To see them whole
To see them desiring You
To see them caring for others
As You care for them
In this perverse generation
Let them have the heart of Shem

Help me to love at all costs
Help me to pour out my life
Help me to live with my children
Without bickering and strife
Please Lord give me the heart of a mother

Mary pondered in her heart
All You said and did
Mary accepted her lot in life
All the reproach all the rejection
heartache and suffering
Please Lord give me the heart of a mother

She endured the pain when You were born
She was there to watch You die
The pain endured at that time no one can deny
Oh such love
Please Lord give me the heart of a mother

Please help me to understand the hurting
Please help me to comfort
Please help me not to think of myself
Please help me to pour out my life
Please Lord give me the heart of a mother

ARE WE THERE YET

I am not saying this because I am in need,
for I have learned to be content whatever the circumstances.
Philippians 4:11

In the month of August, 1998, we were driving to Los Angeles to visit with friends, Jeff and his family. Jeff had lived with us in the community for eight years as a single brother and we were looking forward to being with him again. Ephraim and Tally, two teenage boys from Israel, were traveling with us. We had known their parents for twenty years and to me we were family.

During our journey, Tally told us a story: A family was taking a long excursion to visit their relatives. The father gave clear instructions to his youngest son, "This car ride is going to take a very long time. We will not get to grandma's house till it gets dark. I don't want you to ask me every five minutes, 'Are we there yet?'" They put their luggage in the trunk, fastened their seat belts and began their long drive to grandma's house. About ten minutes had passed when the father felt a tapping on his shoulder. His youngest son asked, "When is it going to get dark?"

It reminded me of a visit with Scott and Beth in Florida. It was their tenth wedding anniversary, and we were watching the children while they took a second honeymoon in Barbados. It was special spending time with our grandchildren again, and I learned a valuable lesson while baby-sitting.

One morning, we decided to take the children to the beach. A short while after we arrived, Joseph came to me and asked, "Nana, can we go home now?" I encouraged him to enjoy the beach while we were still there. As he ran back to Shelly, who was with Emily in the ocean, the Lord reminded me how the children were always looking to the next happening.

If we were at the house, they would ask, "Can we go to the beach?" Here at the beach, Joseph asked, "Can we go home now?" When eating at home, the children would ask, "Why can't we go out to eat?" While playing a game together, inevitably one of the children would ask, "Nana, can you color with me?"

The still small voice of the Lord spoke to my heart, "That's just like you. These past years you have been asking Me, 'What's next?' Why are you always asking Me, 'What do you want me to do?' Do what is set before you now, with all of your heart. In every situation you find yourself, learn to trust Me with your whole heart."

Can you relate? Shelly and I had not received clear direction since the church split. We had been living from house-to-house and leasing the church building month-to-month. Everything surrounding our lives seemed tentative. However, the Lord was asking me to live my life wholeheartedly through every circumstance in Him. My questioning Shelly, if he had heard from the Lord for clear direction, was like asking, "Are we there yet?" The Lord desired to teach me to be content in Him, with a grateful heart, serving Him fervently in everything set before me each day.

> *And whatever you do, whether in word or deed,*
> *do it all in the name of the Lord Jesus,*
> *giving thanks to God the Father through him.*
> Colossians 3:17

⋘⋙

Please teach us to wait for You. Help us to remember that You are a loving Father, transforming us to be more like Jesus. Please guide us with Your eye, and help us to learn how contentment comes:

From The Knowledge Of The Lord

But godliness with contentment is great gain.
I Timothy 6:6

OUR FATHER

I will remain in the world no longer,
but they are still in the world,
and I am coming to you.
Holy Father, protect them by the power of your name —
the name you gave me—
so that they may be one as we are one.
John 17:11

On December 6, 2001, my parents moved from Florida to live with us in our home that we purchased in Scottsdale, Arizona. My father was eighty-eight years old and my mother was eighty-three. Shelly and I had been married for thirty-nine years; I could hardly believe it. The cycle of life became more of a reality to me and I found myself pondering the heart of God for His family.

Jesus had taught us to pray, Our Father. What does that really mean for us today? Who are the ones Jesus taught to pray, Our Father? Do we comprehend what Jesus accomplished for us at the cross? If we could only see clearly what He had accomplished, our lives would never be the same.

Did you ever stop to think that before His resurrection, Jews and Gentiles could not even eat together? Now we can pray together, Our Father. If God is Our Father, that makes us sisters and brothers —*mishpacha,* family. Do we believe that? Do we live according to that truth?

Do we really believe that the Lord is our peace and He has broken down the middle wall of partition between Jew and Gentile? Psalm 133 exhorts us that *it is good and pleasant when brothers dwell together in unity.* God declares in Exodus 4:22 that *Israel is my son, even my first-born.* In the New Testament we read that *to those that received Him, to them gave He power to become the sons of God,* John 1:11.

Tragically, the church has become an organization, holding Sunday and mid-week services, which does not compensate for her failure to demonstrate *the manifold wisdom of God to rulers and authorities in the heavenly places* according to Ephesians 3:10. Authentic relationships within the church, as well as the church's relationship to God the Father and to the nation Israel, need to be restored.

Israel missed the day of visitation over 2,000 years ago in the person of Jesus, who was *the radiance of God's glory and the exact representation of his being,* as is written in Hebrews 1:3. As a result, Israel will not come to know Jesus as the Messiah, *until the fullness of the Gentiles comes in,* according to Romans 11:25.

In the meantime, the Lord longs to see the manifestation of His life demonstrated to Israel through the church. This can be accomplished by having authentic relationships to one another, and to the Lord.

Each one of us has a special place in the heart of the Lord, just as each child has a special place in their parents' heart. How do parents feel when their children are at odds with each other, or with them? Have we ever stopped to think about the ache in the heart of Our Father when His children are not one in Him? That was the Lord's heart and prayer for all, *that they may be one, just as We are one;* from John 17:22. (New American Standard)

On the church property at Calvary, there was a fruit tree that stood between the sanctuary and the fellowship hall. On the day that Shelly was prayed in as pastor, I walked to the fellowship hall and as I approached the fruit tree, the still small voice told me to look up. I remember looking up and wondering what it was that I was supposed to see. His voice was persistent in telling me to look. I began to look more closely at the fruit.

I was shocked when I realized that lemons and oranges were growing on the fruit tree, together. By the natural eye, we could never know if it was the oranges or the lemons that were grafted into the original tree. The oranges still appeared as oranges and the lemons looked like lemons; however, they were both being fed and sustained by the same root.

I, Jesus, have sent my angel
to give you this testimony
for the churches.
I am the Root
and the Offspring of David...
Revelation 22:16

The Lord then spoke to my heart that it was His desire that Jews and Gentiles would dwell together on that property in peace, being guided and fed by Him. His desire was for us to love each other and to live for His glory.

This is also a picture of what God desires for His people, the church, both Jew and Gentile being one in Him together being nourished by Him. We might look different and even sound different. Remember, we Jews are a peculiar people. While the lemons still appeared to be lemons and the oranges appeared to be oranges, they were being fed by the same root, on the same tree.

The family of God transcends the natural cultures that we have been brought up in and should demonstrate the kingdom of God here on earth. It begins by living by the two greatest commandments:

... Love the Lord your God
with all your heart
and with all your soul
and with all your mind.
This is the first
and greatest commandment.
And the second is like it:

279

Love your neighbor as yourself.
Matthew 22:37 - 39

The *ecclesia*, the called out ones are the church, people that are in fellowship with one another, being led by one Lord to establish His Kingdom. As Americans, it is virtually impossible for us to understand what it is to live in a kingdom. We do not have a king. We elect the man we want to be the leader. If we lived elsewhere, we might have a little better understanding of the love or admiration one has for royalty, one birthed into the family not by the choice of man, but by the will of God.

I believe the Lord is waiting for us as His children to allow Him to be our Master, our Father, our Teacher and our King. I know that it begins with my heart first, just as it begins with your heart. The Lord has enabled us to have the power to become the children of God and to be reconciled to Him. He is waiting for us, as His children, to be reconciled to one another.

When we look at all the descriptions of God as Father, we see believers are called sons and daughters, the Messiah is called the bridegroom, the church is called the bride and Israel is called the Lord's wife. All these terms speak of intimate family relationships.

The sooner we return to God's divine way, the sooner we will become a powerful demonstration to a lost and dying world.

❧

Our Father, I pray that you will enable us all to enter into Your heavenly Kingdom with one heart and one mind. Help me, Lord, to live my life as Your daughter. I look forward to the day that Your children are reconciled to You and to one another. Help me, Lord, to be faithful and true to You and to my brothers and sisters. I thank You, Lord, because You will complete what you have begun, both in the church and for Israel.

Just as our natural body functions in unity, so should the spiritual body of Messiah. Pray for the Lord to enlighten your eyes and mind. Pray for the Spirit of unity to come—within the church.

Demonstrate The Family Of God Through Your Life

For this reason I bow my knees before the Father,
from whom every family in heaven
and on earth derives its name,
that He would grant you,
according to the riches of His glory,
to be strengthened with power through His Spirit
in your inner man;
so that Christ (Messiah)
may dwell in your hearts through faith;
and that you, being rooted and grounded in love,
may be able to comprehend with all the saints
what is the breadth and length
and height and depth,
and to know the love of Christ, (Messiah)
which surpasses knowledge,
that you may be filled up
to all the fullness of God.
Now to Him who is able to do
exceeding abundantly
Beyond all that we ask or think,
According to the power that works within us.
To Him be the glory in the church
and in Christ (Messiah) Jesus
to all generations for ever and ever.
Amen.
Ephesians 3:14-21 (Brackets added)

My Dad

SHALOM DAD

He said,
"Surely they are my people,
sons who will not be false to me;"
and so he became their Savior.
Isaiah 63:8

When my mother phoned from Florida to ask for help because my father suffered with Alzheimer's, and she was in need of dialysis treatments, I panicked. How would I handle their moving in with us? Was my heart prepared to take care of them? Would their moving to Phoenix be their salvation? Help, Lord!

I paced back and forth on our back patio crying out to the Lord, "Where should I look for help? How am I to handle this situation? What if we go on a ministry trip to another country, who will take care of my parents? Where will we get the funds needed to pay for their care? What am I to do, Lord?"

I became even more unsettled with the Lord's response, "You are to do nothing!" I cried, "Do nothing? What do you mean, Lord? How can I do nothing? How am I going to be able to take care of all my responsibilities as a mother, grandmother and a pastor's wife and care for my parents? How can I do nothing?"

In the gentle tender way of the Lord, in His still small voice, He spoke these words: "I will take care of everything, June. But remember one thing. Do not go into their world, you stay in Me."

My heart was settled. I could trust the Lord to take care of everything, just as He had promised. The following Scripture was then on my mind and placed deep within my heart:

*You will keep in perfect peace
him whose mind is steadfast,
because he trusts in you.*
Isaiah 26:3

These past years have brought many trials and tests that came from within and from without. However, the Lord continued to show Himself faithful to me as I remembered and kept His words, *"Stay in Me."* Whenever I felt as though I would faint, the Lord raised me up. My heart was being changed as the pressures mounted around me.

My relationship with my father had always been a difficult one. We had a history. He had served in the army during World War II and was stationed in Juno, Alaska. That is how I received my name.

My mother's pregnancy with me presented a problem because my parents were secretly married. All American civilians related to the armed forces had been ordered to leave Alaska. Juno is close to the Aleutian Islands, and the United States was preparing for a possible invasion by Japanese troops.

My mother tried to terminate her pregnancy so that she could remain in Alaska with my father. She tried jumping off the refrigerator, taking hot baths and going horse back riding. When nothing worked, my father confessed to his sergeant that he was secretly married, realizing that the army would pay for my mother's flight back to the states.

As a result, my father was court marshaled. Rather than going to jail, he opted for their punishment which was to dig an eight-foot square hole in the ground. My father was barely 5'2" with his shoes on. They had to pull him out of the hole after digging six square feet. I caused a problem for my father before I was even born.

When I was two years old, the war ended. My father was stationed in Seattle, Washington, and my mother and I flew there to be with him. He wanted his bride and a belated honey moon, but there I was, causing him a problem once again.

My mother told me that I had a secret friend in Seattle. I spent all my time talking and playing with him, while my parents were together in the evenings. I would not eat until my mother put food on a plate and set it on the table for my secret friend. My secret friend's name was Shiloh. Recently, I was reminded of my secret friend and it was then that I realized that Shiloh is one of the names of the Lord.

During my growing up years, I always felt as though I was in my father's way. He never held me on his lap or kissed me. He never demonstrated any fatherly affection to me. My father was also unable to demonstrate affection to my mother as well. There were incidents in my teen years with my father that were very painful.

There was a period of almost a year when he would not even speak to me. That was a time of great suffering for me. I remember going to a counselor with him and my mother who encouraged my father to talk with me. And he did.

After I married Shelly, our relationship improved some; however, I always sensed my father's disdain for me. It was very difficult for my father when my parents moved to Phoenix.

However, over the years living with us, my father's heart was graciously changed by the Lord. He became very thankful for being with us and conveyed his love for me. On many occasions in the year before he went home to be with the Lord, he would verbally bless Shelly and bless me for taking care of him and my mother.

I can still picture him as I write, sitting in the dining room saying, "God bless you. God bless you for all you are doing for us." In all the years of my life, my father had never pronounced a blessing over me until …

One day, as I was preparing lunch for my father, while my mother was having a dialysis treatment, he asked to speak with me. He wanted me to know that I was always his favorite. I was so surprised to hear those words that I asked him if he knew who it was that he was speaking to, and he replied, "Yes. I am speaking to my daughter, June."

He looked so old and frail as he was talking with me. My heart went out to him as he spoke. He asked me to forgive him and as tears filled my eyes, I forgave my father. In a moment of time, the Lord healed the hurt that was deep within my heart. My father then said that he was very tired as he walked slowly to his room. He had made his peace with me, and in my heart I knew that He would soon see the Prince of Peace, His Messiah.

The final days of my father's life were spent in our home. He had been released from the hospital in the final stages of emphysema. Our family came to say their good-byes.

One afternoon I called out for Shelly to come to my father's bedside; his breathing had changed dramatically. Shelly knelt by his bed and took his hand and prayed, as I got on the bed next to my father and held his other hand.

Tears streamed down my cheeks as I said, "*Shalom,* Dad." My dad lifted his head slightly from his pillow and gave up his last breath. That was on Sunday, December 21, 2003 at 3 p.m. Peace filled the bedroom as my father was ushered into the world to come.

❧❧

Only the presence and the love of God can change a man's heart. If you have suffered rejection from your father, may you experience God's healing touch even now. May you receive, by revelation, the everlasting love and care that our Father in heaven has for you.

May The Blessing Of The Lord Be Upon You

LORD, you establish peace for us;
all that we have accomplished
you have done for us.
Isaiah 26:12

Family

Father Mother Sister Brother
Children Cousins Aunts Uncles
Grandparents Grandchildren
Nieces Nephews
Family

Love is all encompassing
Hearts are fulfilled
Times together remembered
And cherished
Family

Lord bring the day about
When families are restored to You
Revival come to our families
Renewed love and appreciation for one another
Worship of God in truth together
Family

Honesty Loyalty Reality
Truth Prevailing Fellowship
Light Love Rejoicing
Laughing Playing Singing
Times together to be cherished
Family

Fill our hearts with Your love Lord
Open our eyes to Your point of view
Open our ears to hear Your voice
Direct our steps to walk in Your Ways
Anoint our hands to bring Your comfort to
Our Family

Help us to do Your will
And above all
Bring honor to Your Son
Make our family one
In You Lord
Amen

Mom
Nana June

June Volk

HILLY

I am bringing my righteousness near, it is not far away;
and my salvation will not be delayed.
I will grant salvation to Zion, my splendor to Israel.
Isaiah 46:13

On Mother's Day of 2005, Debbie, a Jewish believer from Tennessee, came for a visit. She showed me pictures of two Israeli girls coming to Phoenix as exchange students. She believed Shelly and I should host one. I looked at the pictures and Hilly touched my heart deeply. However, all of our children had moved to Charlotte, North Carolina. My mother was in poor health. I immediately dismissed the idea. It was out of season to host an exchange student. So I thought.

About one month later, I received a phone call from the Phoenix leader of the exchange student program. She thought Shelly and I should host Hilly. I explained our living situation, but she would not take no for an answer. We reluctantly agreed to be interviewed.

My mother took a bad fall and split her head open and badly sprained her ankle. I phoned Leslie to say this was not the season for us to host a student. She was persistent.

Shelly and I prayed for wisdom. We decided to explain in a welcome letter to Hilly that we were Messianic Jews. If she and her parents agreed for us to host Hilly, we would know it was the will of God. It was also against the Israeli exchange student policy for Messianic Jews to be the host family for an Israeli exchange student. It would take a miracle.

One Sunday morning, in August of 2005, Hilly arrived in Phoenix. Scott and his family were visiting, so Beth, Alysa and Emily came with me to the airport to welcome Hilly. We all fell in love with her. She immediately became part of our family.

Hilly was an artist and flutist. She was enrolled in a charter school that specialized in music and art. The school was a half hour from our home and within a week, Hilly was very disappointed in their scholastic program. We were told it would be impossible for her to switch schools. However, we discovered the Jesse Schwartz Jewish High School was five minutes from our home.

Leslie, the exchange student leader in Phoenix, phoned the school and was surprised when they set up an interview for the following morning. Within five minutes of the interview, I asked how Hilly could be a student. After they tested her, they offered a full tuition scholarship that was worth $12,000. The Jesse Schwartz Jewish High School was a provision from God.

Hilly had begun to read the New Testament in Israel and she had many questions about the new covenant. She did not know if God existed, but her heart was open to the God of Israel. I loved talking with her about the Lord. She sat in at our Bible studies in our home. She followed the readings in her Hebrew Bible. I loved watching her, as she listened to our discussions on Judges and First Samuel.

Hilly was delightful. She brought new life to me and I loved her as a daughter and friend. Hilly brought much joy to my mother and Shelly as well. We celebrated *Shabbat* and lit candles in the ceramic clay holders that her mother, Nadine, had made for us. We had many guests for *Shabbat* dinners and they were truly memorable times.

Hilly's mother was a Moroccan Jew. Her father was a Romanian Jew and his parents were Holocaust survivors. Shelly and I had been in close relationship with Pentecostal leaders in the northern part of Romania for many years. They had asked us to visit for a long time and perhaps this was the season. We had a problem though, our finances.

If we were to go to Romania, I thought Hilly should come with us. She overheard a conversation about funds, so she told me not even to consider taking her. I assured Hilly that if she was to accompany us, God would provide the funds. She asked, "How would you know it was God?" I told her, "If God provided the funds, even you would know it is His provision." Sure enough, Shelly checked United Airlines thinking we might have a free ticket. And so it was. Hilly came with us to Romania, free of charge.

We were concerned that Hilly would be bored living with us. Were we ever surprised. God had plans for Hilly to travel in America, Romania and Mexico. He had plans for her to have extended family in America and Romania.

During her winter break, we flew to Washington, D.C. and stayed with our old friends whom Hilly came to love. Touring the capital and laughing together are memories that will last a life time. Our friend, Bea, gave Hilly her beautiful full length suede fur lined coat for Romania. Hilly lives in the southern most part of Israel. She did not have the proper clothing for forty below zero. Incidentally, the suede coat is now in Romania covering Gabi, the wife of an evangelist. Hilly experienced the provision of God. Bea also gave us funds that covered one of our tickets to Romania.

We then drove to Charlotte to be with our children to celebrate Christmas and Hilly's seventeenth birthday, December 25. From ice skating to family times around the table, watching movies and playing games, laughing, talking, singing and praising the Lord at Scott's congregation, are memories to be cherished.

Our time together in Romania was another touch from the Lord into Hilly's life. From Nicu, Lidia and their children, the family we stayed with, to all the people she met, Hilly experienced the love of her Messiah. The opportunities she had, helping care for orphans and children from remote villages, were also experiences that will remain with her always. Hilly was family to all she came in contact with. She loved her time in her father's homeland and we loved having her with us.

Hilly had the opportunity to travel to California with her Israeli classmates and their families. She also went to an orphanage in Mexico with our congregation. She loved playing her flute with

291

the children in Mexico. Hilly was growing up with many new and exciting experiences, both here in America and abroad.

My niece, Carrie, had lost her fiancé in The Twin Towers on 9/11. She met a wonderful young man named Pete and was to be married during the month of April, in New Jersey. She invited Hilly to her wedding, so this gave us another opportunity to travel with her. Hilly was to return to Israel in early May.

All of our children were at the wedding and we rented a vehicle, planning to take Hilly back to visit Bea in Virginia. On our way, we followed our children's van and our plans changed. We stopped at a restaurant where Scott suggested that since we were so close to Charlotte, why not come for a week to be with our grandchildren. With such an incentive, we spent the next week in Charlotte. Hilly had another opportunity to be with our family before returning home.

We then drove to New York City. The house we were supposed to stay in was no longer available. However, the Lord had made a unique provision, the headquarters of Jews For Jesus, in mid-town Manhattan. From the Jesse Schwartz Jewish High School to Jews For Jesus! Hilly was really getting an education.

A *Hasidic* Jewish couple from Israel were residing in the Jews For Jesus building. They believed in Jesus, so Hilly was able to hear the gospel in Hebrew. And, we were able to park every night for a week on the street, without getting ticketed or being towed away. This is unheard of in New York City.

Shelly and I who are New Yorkers by birth, never saw so much of New York City as we did with Hilly. We walked through Central Park and explored the Metropolitan Museum of Art. Hilly especially enjoyed Chinatown and Greenwich Village. We took the ferry to Ellis Island and Hilly was able to see the Statue of Liberty. It was an awesome experience to visit Ground Zero, very sobering. We also went to Brooklyn and Connecticut, so Hilly could see where we grew up and later lived. In Brooklyn, we had the opportunity to visit a Russian couple who lived in the apartment where I grew up. My old neighborhood was filled with Hasidic Jews; I was overwhelmed.

We spoke with several *Hasidic* women that day, and I was blessed to see how the Lord had preserved my neighborhood with His people.

Finally, it was time for Hilly to return to her homeland. To think that just a year ago, Hilly was not part of our lives and now she was like our daughter. We once thought that she would not have a positive experience in America, being with us. However, by the grace of God, this season has been unforgettable and enriching for us all.

At the airport we embraced at the departure gate, as I whispered in Hilly's ear, not to forget *Hashem Yeshua, Baruch Hashem* (The Name Jesus, Bless the Name).

Hilly e-mailed that when she had left us in the airport she had been drawn to a woman before boarding the plane. They began to converse and after boarding they discovered that their seats were next to each other. Hilly said that she knew I would call this woman, "A real believer!" She sent me the woman's e-mail and we have been corresponding ever since. She, along with her friends in Tel Aviv, pray for Hilly every morning. She gave Hilly a book in Hebrew about an Israeli orthodox Jew who got saved. Hilly said it was just like reading *Ben Israel: Odyssey Of A Modern Jew,* by Arthur Katz. I had given Hilly a copy in Hebrew. The Lord really does take care of that which concerns us. I look forward to the next time we can see Hilly face-to-face. She will always be in our hearts and in our prayers.

∽ॐ∾

If the Lord should require something of you that seems out of season, do it and be blessed. The Lord will make provision for all of your needs; He will show Himself faithful to you. Remember Hilly.

Now unto him that is able
to do exceeding abundantly
above all that we ask or think...
Ephesians 3:20

Only Believe

I make known the end from the beginning,
from ancient times, what is still to come.
I say:
My purpose will stand,
and I will do all that I please.
Isaiah 46:10

Hilly

THE ELEVENTH HOUR

Say to the Daughter of Zion,
"See, your king comes to you, gentle and riding on a donkey,
on a colt, the foal of a donkey."
Matthew 21:5

It had been two and a half years since my Dad was called home. My mother was getting progressively weaker, and her days were very lonely. She spent most of her time watching television or at the dialysis treatment center. After my father's passing, she had many surgeries and she was growing weary.

I loved my mother dearly, and it was difficult for me watching her lose her sight and her desire to live. Her greatest joy in the past years was being the Matron of Honor at my niece Carrie's wedding. She looked beautiful, dressed in her powder blue dress and jacket with her silver shoes and lovely bouquet, as she walked down the aisle. Her face glowed with joy for Carrie and Pete – she was radiant. After she returned home to Phoenix, her desire to die increased.

I had asked the Lord to please not let her take her last breath until she knew Him. My mother was questioning if Jesus was the Messiah. She had trouble believing that God had a son and she told me so. Mom came to the services at Immanuel Congregation and sat in on our Bible studies. On Tuesday mornings, I taught a Bible study to women, about an hour from our home, and she would accompany me. She loved the women, and lunch together at their club was always a treat for her. I had hope in my heart that faith would come to my mother to believe in Jesus, by hearing and hearing by the Word of God.

On Monday, August 7, we had to phone 911 because my mother was having difficulty breathing. She was in the hospital for almost a week. When she returned home, she came to the Bible study with me on Tuesday morning. On Friday morning, August 18, I received a phone call from the dialysis center that they were bringing my mother to the emergency room at the hospital. I panicked! We only had one vehicle at the time and Shelly was not home. I phoned him on his cell and we raced to the hospital.

As we pulled into the parking lot, they were wheeling my mother out of the ambulance into the emergency room. I ran out of the car and took my mother's hand to let her know that I was there. All she could say was, "Pain, pain, pain." My mother was having a heart attack. Shelly and I held her hands. Shelly tried to encourage her to call out to the Lord for help. He told her that she really needed Him and the Lord desired to help her. Gritting her teeth, my mother responded, "I can't talk." My heart hurt for her. Why would she not call out for help to the only One who could help her now?

The male nurse tending her told us that they had shocked her heart at the dialysis center. He could not understand why, since it was written on her papers that she did not want that done. I told him I knew why and he looked at me funny. I told him that I had prayed and asked the Lord not to allow her to take her last breath until she knew Him. He said, "I'll accept that." I thought she would regain her strength, since her heart was so hard.

We were expecting our two youngest granddaughters, Emily and Rachel, on Saturday. All our other grandchildren were going to a Bible camp, so we had decided to fly the two girls to Phoenix for a week. My mother was so looking forward to their visit. She kept apologizing to me when they settled her in a room in ICU. I told her not to worry; she would be home in a few days. I let her know that I would not be at the hospital on Saturday, but I would come on Sunday to fix her hair, so she would look good for the girls.

On Friday evening while doing wash, I went to see if the clothes in the dryer were finished. I took note that there were eleven minutes left on both the washer and the dryer. That night, I had a difficult time sleeping. When I awoke, I looked at the time, the clock read 1:11a.m. Later on Saturday morning, I asked Shelly to look up The Eleventh Hour in the Scriptures. It appears only once and it is found in Matthew Chapter 20. It reads that some come into the kingdom the third hour, some the sixth, some the ninth and some the eleventh hour. I knew the Lord was saying something to me about The Eleventh Hour, but I did not know what it was at that time.

Shelly never misses church. The week before my mother went into the hospital, I had asked Shelly if we could dedicate the time with Emily, Rachel and my mother on Sunday. I asked him if he could have someone else preach. Unlike Shelly, he agreed, without asking a second time. We picked the girls up at the airport on Saturday and Shelly went to see my mother at the hospital, while I got the girls settled at home.

Sunday morning, I drove Shelly and the girls to an amusement park, and I went to the hospital to fix my mother's hair. When I was about two minutes from the hospital, Shelly phoned to tell me the hospital had just called. My mother's lungs were filling up with fluid and her pressure was dropping; he said if I needed him, he would take a taxi to be with me.

As soon as I saw my mother, I knew she was passing-on. I phoned Shelly and asked him to come quickly. I fell to my knees by my mother's bedside, and took her hand in mine. I said, "Mom, I'm here! Mom, I love you. We all love you, Mom. The Lord loves you. Please don't harden your heart; the Lord wants to help you." I cried.

The nurse was so kind; she put a pillow under my knees and asked if I wanted the pulmonary doctor to take fluid from my mother's lungs, she said that it would help her. I wept. I did not know what to do. I knew that my mother was so tired of living and yet, I believed to do everything to save life. What should I do? As I looked at my mother again, I said softly and calmly, "I think she is going." The nurse responded, "I do, too." She walked to the sliding doors and pulled the curtains closed. I was alone in the room with mom. My heart pounded in my chest as I prayed. Lord, please reveal Yourself to Mom before she takes her last breath.

She seemed calmer as her breathing was getting lighter and lighter. My head was down. When I lifted my head I saw a manifestation of darkness holding my mother back from believing. I declared, "You spirit of unbelief, come out of Claire Bernstein now." The manifestation did not leave until I repeated three times, "Come out of Claire Bernstein now!" I asked the Lord for His Spirit to fill my mother with faith to believe—her countenance changed.

Her eyes opened wide; she seemed to be looking at something on the wall. I looked and saw nothing. She moved her eyes back and forth several times as if she was seeing something. She closed her eyes as her breathing was getting lighter and lighter. The nurse returned and moved her monitor. Was my mother gone? The nurse nodded her head. My mom was gone—she was taken home.

I looked at the clock—it was 11:55 a.m. Peace filled the room. An angel or the Lord Himself took my mother, and I knew it. She was taken in the last minutes of The Eleventh Hour.

I phoned Shelly to tell him that Mom was gone. I then phoned our children to tell them that their Grandmother was gone. Dean phoned me back to tell me that his youngest son Jesse, who was twelve-years-old at the time, had a dream that Saturday night about his Great Grandma Clair, my mother:

> *Scott was preaching to a very large crowd, tossing out gifts. Jesse's Grandma Joan, who was a strong believer, was among the crowd. She has been in heaven with the Lord since Trudy was eighteen. Jesse then saw Shelly and me pushing my mother in a high-chair into the place where Scott was preaching. She did not look like Great-Grandma Claire—she was just a baby. Jesse said that when we entered the place where Scott was preaching, everyone in the crowd stood up and cheered for Great Grandma Claire.*

Shelly, Me, and Mom

My Mother Entered the Kingdom of God As A Baby IN THE ELEVENTH HOUR

I went to the funeral home to fix my mother's hair for the last time. I brought her powder blue dress and jacket for her to wear; her matron of honor dress, the one she wore to Carrie's wedding. Jonathan Bernis, the Executive Director of Jewish Voice Ministries, who has led thousands of Jews to the Lord in Russia, blessed us by conducting the funeral service for my mother. He had also directed the funeral service for my father. Thank you, Jonathan. My Mom was laid to rest by my Dad. They are with the Lord forever. They have been reunited in the world to come. And now, they are waiting for us to join them.

My mother's passing reminded me of a Word the Lord gave Shelly and me in Charlotte, in 1978: "If your parents do not acknowledge Me in North Carolina, their hearts will be hardened throughout eternity."

My parents did acknowledge Jesus as Lord in North Carolina. Shelly led them in a prayer of salvation. The answer to their confession of faith was not manifested until their last days on earth.

It was in The Eleventh Hour that God fulfilled His Word to us— their hearts were not hardened throughout eternity. And now, they are with the Lord forever. Thank You, Lord.

ॐॐ

Let your heart be encouraged and trust the Lord for your loved ones. Never lose hope. Keep praying. The Lord desires to bring your loved ones to Him, even in The Eleventh Hour.

Hope In God—He Is Worthy To Be Praised

The workers who were hired about the eleventh hour
came and each received a denarius.
So when those came who were hired first,
they expected to receive more.
But each one of them also received a denarius.
When they received it,
they began to grumble against the landowner.
"These men who were hired last worked only one hour," they said,
"and you have made them equal to us
who have borne the burden of the work
and the heat of the day."
"So the last will be first, and the first will be last."
Matthew 20: 9 - 12, 16

Jesus answered and said to them,
"This is the work of God,
that you believe in Him
whom He has sent."
John 6:29

Unfailing Love

We search with hearts so desirous of acceptance
We see the uncertainty of the age
In which we live
Is there a place of solace
Is there One who loves and forgives

My friend I'm here to comfort you with truth
There is One for whom your soul
Longs to see
He is alive and cares like none other
Truly cares for you and me

Don't stop searching with all your heart
For there you will find
UNFAILING LOVE—In Him
The Lord who truly cares
Who sees all from above

He longs to live within your heart
To commune with you day by day
For in Him there is UNFAILING LOVE
An anchor for your soul—THE ROCK
Your sure stay

June Volk

Conclusion

My Family

Left to right: Scott, Jonathan, Emily, Joseph, Alysa and Beth

Top left to right: Benjamin and Jesse, Dean and Trudy

Top left to right: Sarah, Billy, Timothy. Middle: Bill. Bottom left to right: Rachel and Suzi.

WHERE DO WE GO FROM HERE

And His disciples said to Him,
"You see the multitude pressing in on You, and You say,
Who touched Me?"
Mark 5:31

Since my mother passed on, we believe that a season has passed on for us as well. We are waiting for the new season to begin. The scene, when Jesus asked His disciples, *"Who touched Me,"* while multitudes of people were pressing in on Him, is very descriptive of where we are today. Shelly and I are in the midst of the crowd reaching out to touch the hem of His garments.

It has been twelve long years since the split at Calvary Church of the Valley. The slander in our midst has ceased for which we are eternally grateful. The Lord has healed our hearts, just as the woman who touched the hem of His garments was healed.

I had grown weary and lost all hope for the future. However, the Lord renewed the hope in my heart after meditating on the book of Romans, Chapter 15:1-13. Those verses explain that hope comes through the exhortation of the Scriptures, perseverance, trusting the Lord and by the power of the Holy Spirit. Since hope is not seen, or it would not be hope, we have not yet seen the victory. But we believe that it is coming. Somehow, we know that the Lord has a plan and we are waiting for Him to reveal it to us.

Shelly is now the pastor of Immanuel Congregation, a small group of people loving and seeking the Lord and His kingdom. We have a radio program, "For Zion's Sake," which airs in the Phoenix area each week day morning. I speak at women's conferences and teach Bible studies in Goodyear and Carefree, two suburban areas of Phoenix. Shelly is also a conference speaker as well as a teacher of the Word.

We are in relationship with leaders all over the world, so we have had opportunities to travel and minister to those we love, as well as to their congregations.

We intercede for the unity of the spirit in the Church and for God's Kingdom to come. We also intercede for Israel and our Jewish kinsmen, because our hearts' cry is for our people to come to know Jesus.

Prayer has always been very close to my heart. To see victory come in the lives of those who love the Lord and serve Him is joy unspeakable. To see salvation come to a soul is joy unspeakable. It is worth it all if one little one comes and bows his knee to the King of Kings.

We might not have the answer to Where Do We Go From Here, however, we are confident that the God Who answers by fire knows. That brings a deep comfort to our hearts to wait on Him. He knows that we are pressing in to touch the hem of His garments.

The woman with the blood issue for twelve years, as described in Mark 5, spent all of her money on physicians and no one could help her. But one touch of the hem of His garments, that was all it took for her to be healed.

Jesus knew that someone had pressed in and touched Him among the multitude. Someone touched Him and virtue left Him. So I ask you, are you pressing in to touch the hem of His garments? Where do you go from here?

Where are you? That was the question the Lord asked Adam as He walked in the Garden of Eden. Adam was hiding behind a tree with Eve because they were afraid. They knew they had disobeyed the Lord and were ashamed. Today, the Lord is asking you, where are you? Don't hide as Adam and Eve did. The Lord is waiting for you to press in and touch the hem of His garments. He desires to touch you and to heal your broken heart and to revive your spirit.

In Mark 5:36, 39 Jesus said, *"Do not be afraid any longer, only believe."* He spoke this to a synagogue official who was among the multitude, pressing in to ask Jesus to heal his daughter. He had just learned she had died when Jesus said to him, *the child has not died, but is asleep.* Those gathered at the official's home heard what Jesus said and they laughed at Him. Yet, when Jesus prayed and told her to arise, the twelve-year-old girl was resurrected. She awoke. She came to life.

⋦⋗

Where do you go from here? Have you considered the God Who answers by fire? What hinders you to believe that He Is Jesus? Are you fearful of believing in Him? Where are you? Are you pressing in to touch the hem of His garments?

The Holy One Desires To Touch You

Who touched My garments?
Mark 5:30b

Truth Revealed

Is life an illusion
Is our heart ever satisfied
Can we come to a conclusion
Before we die
Should we even try

Questions—Questions
Are there answers for us to see
Are there absolutes in this world
Or just opinions to be respected
Conjectures made by you or me

If we search with all our heart
To know the truth
Will it be revealed
Or is truth
Forever concealed

Is truth a concept
A philosophy determined
By you or me
Or—could truth be a person
One who desires to set us free

I know of One who walked the earth
And claimed to be the truth
I met Him on a quest for the meaning of this life
He answered when I called out to Him
He delivered me from strife

He is God—our Creator
He is the Beginning and the End
He is the Wounded Healer
He understands our struggles
He desires to meet us at each bend

He is waiting for you to call out to Him
Today if you hear His voice—Do not delay
He is the God of Israel—Jesus the Messiah
The Truth the Life and the Way
The only One able to deliver you from all dismay

He is Truth revealed through revelation
By God our Father in Heaven
Abraham and Sarah met Him—Moses met Him—
Joshua knew Him too
Hannah cried—She believed He would hear
My kinsmen—Call out to Him without fear

Samson's mother saw Him—Her husband saw Him too
Boaz was a picture of our Redeemer
He married Ruth a Moabitess not a Jew
Jesus has called strangers to stand by His side
He is the God of Israel calling for His bride

He is turning again to His chosen people
For His promises are true
Israel shall be a Holy Nation of Priests
For the Lord Himself
Will bring them through

Life is no illusion our hearts can be filled with peace
Truth revealed is the answer to our quest our ills our grief
The God of Abraham Isaac and Jacob
O Lord peace at last
Relief

June Volk

TO MY KINSMEN WITH LOVE

Thus saith the LORD the King of Israel,
and his redeemer the LORD of hosts;
I am the first, and I am the last;
and beside me there is no God.
Isaiah 44:6

My kinsmen, my people, you might be asking yourself what sort of Jew am I? I do not write like a Jew or live like a Jew or believe like a Jew. May I offer this thought for your consideration? I was born a Jew and I am also a Jew born anew. My parents, grandparents and great grandparents on both sides were Jewish. As far back as our family is aware, we are pure Jews.

I live as our people of old lived, by His faith, as the prophet Habakkuk exhorted us to live, Habakkuk 2:4. If Jesus is the Messiah for our people, then how can a true Jew live or believe any other way?

As I awoke early one morning, the Lord spoke to my heart about how our people perceive Him in this day and age – unapproachable, impersonal and distant. Yet, the Holy Scriptures reveal that our Creator desired to have a personal relationship with man. As a young girl growing up in New York City, I was never taught at home, or in our synagogue about having a personal relationship with God. I never even considered that it was possible.

In the very first book of the *Torah*, we read that the Lord God walked and talked with Adam in the Garden of Eden, Genesis 3:8. We see that Noah walked with God, Genesis 6:8, 9b. Abraham and Sarah talked with the Lord and He talked with them, Genesis 18.

311

Jacob wrestled with *a man* and concluded he was wrestling with *God*, Genesis 32:31. All this occurred before Moses was even born and the law given. Samson's parents saw the Lord, Judges 13:22. Hannah cried out to the Lord and He answered her, I Samuel 1:10-22. The Lord called to Samuel, Hannah's son, I Samuel 3. These Scriptures clearly show us that the Lord, the God of Israel, visited and spoke to His people and His people spoke with Him.

In the days of Moses, the Lord appeared to him at the door of the tent of meeting, Exodus 33:8-11. On Mount Sinai, He gave Moses the law, Exodus 34:28-34. When Moses descended from the mount after receiving the commandments, the people asked him to speak to God for them, Exodus 20:15, 16.

How great a desire God has to have a people with whom He can commune. To this very day, as His chosen ones, we have misunderstood His heart. God still desires a personal relationship.

According to Jewish writings, Terah, the father of Abraham, who is the father of our faith, was an idol maker. Can you imagine what would have happened if Abraham believed his father and his teachings about idols? Just think where we would be today if Abraham had not asked God questions and searched for His answers. Abraham was a heathen until he found God. He found God because he sought for Him with all his heart. Do you believe like Abraham?

As Jews, we know that the God of Israel is the Creator and the only true God. But do we search for Him to be in communication with Him? Do we call upon Him? Do we ask Him questions? Do we believe He will answer us? That really is a very Jewish thing to do, according to the Holy Writings.

The following verses are taken directly from The Holy Scriptures According To *The Masoretic Text*:

The Jewish Publication Society Of America

Call unto Me, and I will answer thee,
And will tell thee great things, and hidden,
which thou knowest not.
Jeremiah 33:3

O give thanks unto the LORD,
call upon His name;
Make known His doings among the peoples.
Psalm 105:1

And ye shall seek Me, and find Me
when ye shall search for Me with all your heart.
Jeremiah 29:13

I love them that love me,
And those that seek me earnestly
shall find me.
Proverbs 8:17

Happy are they that keep His testimonies,
That seek Him with a whole heart."
Psalms 119:2

Seek ye the LORD while He may be found,
Call ye upon Him while He is near...
Isaiah 55:6

Seek ye the LORD and His strength;
Seek His face continually.
I Chronicles 16:11

So my people, my fervent prayer for you is to consider the Scriptures and search for the living God. He is the God of our fathers and He is the God of Israel. Search for Him with all your heart, soul, mind and strength. His promise is that He will be found of you. His desire is to be loved by you as in the days of old. Ask the God of our fathers, the God of Abraham, Isaac and Jacob, the God Who answers by fire if Jesus is the Messiah—

He will answer thee, And will tell thee great things, and hidden,
which thou knowest not.
Jeremiah 33:3

Behold, the days come,
saith the LORD,
that I will make a new covenant
with the house of Israel,
and with the house of Judah;
not according to the covenant
that I made with their fathers
in the day that I took them by the hand
to bring them out of the land of Egypt;
forasmuch as they broke My covenant,
although I was a lord over them,
saith the LORD.
But this is the covenant
that I will make with the house of Israel
after those days,
saith the LORD,
I will put My law in their inward parts,
and in their heart will I write it;
and I will be their God,
and they shall be My people;
and they shall teach no more every man his neighbour,
and every man his brother, saying:
" 'Know the LORD;'
for they shall all know Me,
from the least of them unto the greatest of them,"
saith the LORD;
"for I will forgive their iniquity,
and their sin will I remember no more."
Jeremiah 31:31-34

For thus saith the LORD:
"Sing with gladness for Jacob,
And shout at the head of the nations;
Announce ye, praise ye, and say:
'O LORD, save Thy people,
The remnant of Israel.'"
Jeremiah 31:7

∽๑๛

From the Book of Hebrews in the New Covenant

GOD,
AFTER He spoke
long ago to the fathers
in the prophets in many portions
and in many ways,
in these last days
has spoken to us
in His Son,
whom He appointed
heir of all things,
through whom also
He made the world.
And He is the radiance
of His glory
and the exact representation
of His nature,
and upholds
all things
by the word
of His power.

When He had made
purification of sins,
He sat down
at the right hand
of the Majesty on high ...
Hebrews 1:1-3

THE LORD IS WAITING FOR YOU
TO CALL OUT TO HIM

Dear *Yeshua*, through revelation knowledge, please, reveal Yourself to every reader of this book as the Holy One of Israel, the Messiah, the Son of the Living God and the Savior of the world.

IN MEMORIAM

*O the depth of the riches both of the wisdom
and knowledge of God!
How unsearchable are his judgments,
and his ways past finding out!
For who hath known the mind of the Lord? Or who hath been
his counsellor? Or who hath first given to him, and it shall be
recompensed unto him again? For of him, and through him, and to
him are all things: To Whom be Glory Forever. Amen*
Romans 11:33-36

Arthur Katz passed on into Glory on June 28, 2007 and the earth lost a great prophetic voice and a father in the faith to countless numbers of Jewish believers.

A privilege the Lord afforded Shelly and Scott was to be fathered by Arthur into the kingdom of God, and in the foundations of the faith. Arthur was a man jealous for authenticity, truth in the inward parts, and was passionate to see the purposes of God fulfilled in the lives of those who called upon the Name of the Lord.

I have personally experienced Arthur weeping in deep travail over the condition of his own life, as well as the condition of the people Israel, and the condition of the Church.

In the last years of Arthur's life he suffered in his physical body. Several months before his departure, Inger took some time apart to be refreshed and strengthened in the Lord while Shelly and I tended to him. Arthur amazed us with his stamina displayed in his diligence in the Word, prayer, meeting with the community of believers living on the property of Ben Israel, as well as his communication by phone with saints from all over the world.

Shelly was scheduled to speak to students attending a discipleship school in Canada one of the Saturday mornings we were caring for him. Arthur was well enough to join with us for the meeting, and we realized that neither Shelly nor I should speak to the students.

The car ride to Canada was long and grueling, but Arthur did well. When we arrived the students graciously welcomed us. The presence of the Lord filled the house, and there was a deep sense of expectancy before the formal meeting began.

Arthur shared his deepest love and burden, the mystery of Jesus, Israel and the Church. He spoke about the weakness of the Church today because of its failure to reach out to the Jews all over the world, taking heed to Apostle Paul's writings to bring the Gospel to the Jew first and also to the Greek. He explained with clarity the tension that keeps a human body healthy and why that tension was missing from the Church today. The conflicts the Church would be forced to face by fulfilling their call to Israel and to the Jews would conclude in strengthening the body of Christ.

Israel in her hardness against Jesus being Messiah and Lord —if not being confronted by the Church today—the Church would remain in her weakened condition.

The call of the Lord, according to the Scriptures to the Church, is being circumvented. The power and authority of Romans 9-11, as well as the writings of the prophets, was expounded by Arthur. There was a hope deep within his heart for the students to 'catch' *this* vision. It caused a stirring within Shelly and within me to see the Biblical Roots of the faith restored to the Church once again.

The passion of Arthur's heart was for the apostolic vision of the first century Church to be restored in the lives of God's people.

His message to the Church was for it to be utterly different— utterly the Lord's—to cry out to know Him—to know His heart— His mind—His desires—to seek after His purposes—not our own. This was the purpose for which Arthur lived.

We will miss him; the Church will miss the voice in the wilderness that Arthur represented. He was wholeheartedly dedicated to see the purposes of God fulfilled in his own life, and in the lives of the saints. His passion for the Church and for the people Israel still cries out in both his vocal messages and in his books as well as in the lives of the ones who knew him and loved him.

The message Arthur spoke in Canada was his last public speaking.

∽⭕⭕∼

A MAN AFTER GOD'S OWN HEART

SO HE WENT AND DID
ACCORDING TO THE WORD OF THE LORD...
I Kings 17:5